DEAR DAUGHTER
OF A
NARCISSISTIC
MOTHER

DEAR DAUGHTER OF A NARCISSISTIC MOTHER

100 LETTERS FOR YOUR HEALING AND THRIVING

DANU MORRIGAN

AUGSBURG BOOKS
MINNEAPOLIS

DEAR DAUGHTER OF A NARCISSISTIC MOTHER
100 Letters for Your Healing and Thriving

Originally published by Darton, Longman and Todd, London, UK
Copyright © 2012 Danu Morrigan

Cover image: Zikatuha / shutterstock
Cover design: Cindy Laun

Print ISBN: 978-1-5064-6213-4
eBook ISBN: 978-1-5064-6213-4

CONTENTS

Why Narcissists Are Never Wrong 164

What Narcissists Will Never Experience 166

What If She Really Does Change? 168

Narcissists as Victims 170

Why Can't You Take Criticism? 172

What about When She's Old? 176

What about Feeling Compassion for Her? 179

What Does Japanese Pottery Have to Do with Being a DONM? 181

"Stop the Silliness" 183

Some Thoughts on Resolving Relationship Issues 185

The Two-Sides Fallacy 187

"But She Wants Me Back! Doesn't That Mean She Loves Me?" 189

What about Drama Queens? 192

We Are the Bonsai Children 195

The Quest for Her Approval 198

What Do Toddlers and Narcissists Have in Common? 201

When People Gush about How Nice She Is, What Do You Do? 203

So How *Do* You Explain Narcissistic Mothers? 205

How Do We Know What the Truth Is? 207

How We Can Get Stuck in the Drama Triangle 211

Some Ideas about How to Step Off the Drama Triangle 214

DEAR FELLOW DAUGHTER
OF A NARCISSISTIC MOTHER

For the past two years I have sent a weekly email letter to thousands of women who, like you, are the daughter of a narcissistic mother. These letters aim to support, encourage, inform, and validate these women, and the regular feedback I receive shows the value they get out of them (see some of the feedback below).

This book is the compilation of those letters, a full one hundred letters in all, and I hope and intend that this book will likewise support, encourage, inform, and validate you.

Although these letters expand on the information on my website (daughtersofnarcissisticmothers.com) and in my book *You're Not Crazy–It's Your Mother*, they do stand alone. So if this is the first of my work you've read, you will still get full value from it.

My hope and intention are that these letters will be your roadmap, guide, and even friend on your journey to full healing from your toxic upbringing, and to thriving in your life going forward.

Here is a sample of the value other daughters of narcissistic mothers have gotten from these letters:

"The letters are coming out in a book? That's great!!!!! I would like to have the letters to read over for meditation. I learn something every time I go back and reread them." Anonymous by request

"Your site and your weekly letters have been not only empowering, but incredibly vindicating. I won't say I couldn't have done it without them, but they certainly helped conceive my rebirth and encourage it to grow and flourish." CHS, Santa Ana

"I find your descriptions of specific details and emotional landscape are really enlightening and validating for the type of emotions and experiences I encounter, which I may not be realizing myself, because of the usual mental unclarity, confusion, fog, and such things. You put names and words and meaning to these experiences, and that is so useful, like a breeze of air in a stuffy room." Alevtina, Kiev, Ukraine

"Your letters have been a godsend. I can't tell you how much they have helped me." S.D.

So, who am I, and why would you listen to me?

I am a fellow daughter of a narcissistic mother (DONM, as we refer to it for shorthand). I have no professional qualifications in anything to do with this topic, so I do not talk down to you from any academic pedestal. Instead, I come to you from the trenches of the lived experience. I'm still on this journey, and I have lots to learn and many roads to take yet. But I have corresponded with thousands of DONMs over the last eight years, and ran a forum for four of those, during which I learned so much about the DONM experience. This hard-earned information is what I share with you.

Also, as a professional writer, my job is to present information in a way that makes sense, and that's what I offer. Many, many DONMs tell me that I explain their experiences—their confusing, bewildering, hard-to-understand experiences—in a way that makes sense to them for the first time. As more than one DONM has told me, "You explain my life to me in a way I never could."

I hope and trust I can do the same for you in the following letters.

Hugs,
Danu

INTRODUCTION

I truly believe that healing and thriving are possible for those of us who were unfortunate enough to be raised by a mother with narcissistic personality disorder (NPD). We are not on an easy journey, for sure, and it's unfair that we have to work so hard just to get to a place where other women—those who had loving mothers—started. But that's the way it is, and we deserve to have all the resources we need to help us as we travel.

I invite you to consider, acknowledge, applaud, and even celebrate your sheer courage. Most people can never bring themselves to examine whether their relationship with their mother is toxic. That you have done so is a huge step, and truly, I do hope you're so proud of yourself for having done that.

Until you acknowledged the toxicity of the way your mother raised you and still treats you, no change was possible. Now that you have acknowledged this huge truth, all things become possible.

Having said that, if you're like many DONMs, you might still be struggling to really accept that she was (and is) indeed toxic. It's not surprising, is it?—given that she probably spent years telling you that she was perfect and that everything was all your fault, that you were overreacting or oversensitive.

I'm still on this journey myself, but I have been on it for a good number of years, many of them before I knew about NPD.

At that time, I thought I was fixing a flawed me, rather than healing an injured me. The same is true for you: you are injured and requiring healing, rather than flawed and requiring fixing as she told you.

Now, what I share here are my own opinions, perceptions, and understandings. They are based on those years of searching and learning and communication with thousands of DONMs, and are my best shot at figuring it all out. But please, please, judge everything I say on its own merits, not because I said it. I am only a fellow traveler, and I share my thoughts, but they're not holy writ or anything like it.

That said, don't automatically dismiss what I say either. Sometimes what you believe and "know" isn't true. It's the residue of your narcissistic mother's brainwashing. Those false beliefs can lead you to dismiss anything contrary to that brainwashing. Indeed, often the more important it is for you to hear something, the more vehemently your existing beliefs will make you dismiss it.

But here's the thing: You need a new way of thinking and of being in the world, as part of your "freeDONM." The old way is your mother's way, and that's not working for you or you wouldn't be seeking answers. So, don't automatically dismiss what I write. I didn't pull it out of nowhere; a lot of thought and learning and thinking and exploring went into all that I say, and there may well be value in it for you. But neither should you accept it uncritically. I do my very best to share good information and accurate perceptions, but I could be wrong about any or all of it. So, be open-minded and don't automatically reject what I write, but don't automatically accept it either. Judge it on its own merits, as I said.

One major tool I'll be referring to again and again is the emotional freedom technique (EFT). EFT has literally changed my life for the better, and I am so excited to share it with you. It is a process of tapping on acupuncture points to release, erase, and evaporate negative emotions and limiting beliefs. This has huge benefits for us, as you'll see. I invite you to visit my website at www

.daughtersofnarcissisticmothers.com/emotional-freedom-technique/ to learn more about it and get the free instructions there.

In each letter I speak of different issues DONMs face, and for many of them I recommend EFT, as so many of our challenges are caused by our limiting emotions and beliefs.

Having said that, I want you to get value out of these letters even if you decide not to even try EFT, so I do my best to offer other alternatives too. In each case the alternative would be, in my opinion, slower and clumsier than EFT, simply because EFT is so quick and efficient, but I do want to give you the choice.

I am honored that you are walking this part of the journey with me, and I hope and trust that it will be a good one.

Hugs,
Danu

ARE YOU A BIRD TRAPPED AGAINST A WINDOW?

Dear DONM,

You know that famous phrase about the definition of madness? It's to keep on doing the same things but expecting a different result.

We DONMs do that with our mothers. We keep going to her hoping that this time it'll be different. This time she'll be the mother we need her to be. This time she'll surely support us in our grief, applaud us in our success, accept us for who we are with no agenda.

And she never does.

When I think of this dynamic (which I, too, did for far too many years), I think of a bird flying fruitlessly into a window, again and again.

It breaks my heart. It breaks my heart for me, and for all of us.

I understand this pattern, and I forgive myself for doing it, as I hope you can forgive yourself.

It's totally natural to want our mothers to love us, so no wonder we keep trying, especially since we believed her constant message that she was perfect and that we were the ones so flawed that it caused all the problems. It made sense that we were the ones who held the solution to fixing the dysfunctional relationship.

But that was a lie, wasn't it? A big, fat, totally nasty lie.

The problem in the relationship lies in no flaw in us, but in the fact that she has narcissistic personality disorder. The fact is that narcissists cannot change and will not change and cannot even see that there is anything to change.

You might know that rationally but not know it deep down, where it counts, where you need to know it.

However, the sooner we realize this truth—really, deep down, at the core of us—the sooner we are truly free.

Once you accept this truth, you are free to make healthy decisions about your life, and we'll be exploring many of those options later.

You'll free up more energy than you ever thought possible: all that energy that is currently wasted flying into that window will be freed up for you to use for your healing and then for your thriving. That freedom is priceless, and it is only a decision away.

Okay, making that decision is not easy. Try journaling about it, or using affirmations, or maybe discuss it with your therapist. Or use EFT. EFT is perfect for taking what you know rationally and making it a core, deep-down belief. You end up feeling that it's true in all of your body, as well as just knowing it's true in your head.

When you let go of the useless hope that your narcissistic mother will change, you free yourself from constantly flying into that window. You stop trying to do the impossible, and that will give you time and energy to start creating the possible: in other words, your own life, lived your way.

I fervently have that wish for you, and for all of us DONMs.

Hugs,
Danu

SURFING YOUR ANGER

Dear DONM,

Note: As we are discussing how to experience and process anger, I share tools such as EFT/tapping, which I fully believe are safe. But you need to know that you are totally accepting responsibility for your use of, and experience with, these tools.

Often when you finally acknowledge and accept the abuse that was done to you, you can experience anger. Rage, even. Fury like you have never known before, to a depth you didn't realize you could manifest.

This rage will probably take you by surprise and may feel overwhelming and intimidating. You probably are not used to it as you, no doubt, were not allowed to express any anger.

What's happening is that your mother-imposed filters have been removed and you are now seeing clearly for the first time and you realize that—hell, yes!—what she did to you was wrong. Beyond wrong, even. All that suppressed anger is coming up to be experienced.

This is good news! I know it feels scary and perhaps even out of control and overwhelming, as I said. But bear with it. I'll give you ideas in a minute for how to process it. But for now, just bear with the anger . . . just let it be . . . just allow it. It won't overwhelm you, no matter how it feels like it might.

This anger is righteous anger. You have every right to be angry at the injustices and abuse that were heaped upon you.

Along with this anger might come fantasies and/or dreams of doing her (them?) violence.

It shocked me when it happened to me. Here I was (am!), a pacifist, a genuinely kind gentle soul, and yet I was having the most incredibly graphic and detailed visions of the violence I could do to both my parents.

I've thought a lot about this, and this is what I've come up with: I think those fantasies and dreams are okay. Maybe they're even necessary for healing.

When we were children, we were powerless against our abusers, but these fantasies allow us to reclaim our power. And the subconscious mind does not distinguish between reality and fantasy, so as far as it's concerned, you have reclaimed your power by doing this.

Now, needless to say, it is not right to act out these fantasies. No one is advocating that you visit actual violence on your parents, or on anyone. That would be wrong on so many levels. It would be legally and morally wrong, of course, but also wrong for *you*. Your healing does not consist of you sinking to their level. I believe it's true that the best revenge is living well, and you becoming a violent person is not living well. Doing actual violence would trap you in their dysfunction.

So don't do it.

But if your brain is bringing up fantasies or dreams, go with them, I suggest. In every case I have heard of, when other DONMs went through this, those thoughts passed in time, with no effort. It seemed to be a process that had to be gone through on the path to healing.

I think the violent thoughts bring the narcissists down to size in our heads. They certainly did in mine. Before that, the narcissists loomed big and scary, as they did when I was a child. They had power over me. Now that I *know* I can physically beat them, they seem small and scared. Pathetic, even. They have no power over me anymore, and that is so freeing.

The thing that we sometimes don't realize about anger is that it's our friend. It's a voice tugging on our sleeve saying, "Er, somebody is mistreating you now." The problem is when we cannot heed that voice. The anger then gets suppressed and gets carried around with us until it's released. This repressed anger is a huge burden to carry. At the very least, it takes a lot of energy to keep it pushed down—energy that could be used for other things, from dancing to building a life.

It is absolutely right and appropriate that this anger be felt and experienced and expressed and processed. And as part of that processing, it moves on. It needs to move on to be healthy. Anger that you are dwelling in, or swimming in, is just as unhealthy as anger that is repressed (arguably, more so indeed).

So, what can you do to process it and move it on?

Just go with it. Accept it and enjoy the ride. Try to embrace it if you can: think of it like you're surfing the biggest, baddest wave you can, and it's equal parts fear and exhilaration. In the act of feeling it and experiencing it and acknowledging it, you are processing it.

Try to find the power in the anger. Only powerful people can afford to get angry, so this isn't a trick; it's real.

Know that it'll take the time it takes. I know that I said not to dwell in or swim in the anger, and that's true. But there is a lifetime of anger there, so it'll take as long as it takes to process it.

There are ways of speeding it up, though:

Maybe write out your anger—do freewriting perhaps—I share more about this in the next letter.

Use EFT. Just tap the points over and over while you are experiencing the anger. It might not feel like anything is happening, but it is working to process and move that chapter of the anger on.

Even better, speak aloud as you tap. Speak whatever comes into your mind. Be as violent and aggressive as you need. Tap each statement on one point and move on to the next. For example: "I hate her—I HATE what she did to me—She's a ******* bitch—How DARE she do that to me?—Oh, God, it hurts what she did to me—I'd like to kill her now."

Even better still, walk while you're doing this. Just pace the room. There is something so empowering and healing about the kinesthetic feeling of moving while you do the tapping and the speaking aloud. You can also tap and walk but not speak aloud, if speaking is not appropriate at the moment. The most powerful, however, is to do all three.

After a while—half an hour maybe; perhaps an hour—you will feel the anger disperse and you will have a kind of exhausted peace. That "chapter" of anger is gone now, never to return. There will be other "chapters," until the anger is all gone, but you've done good work here.

Hugs,
Danu

ANOTHER FREE, WONDERFUL
TOOL FOR HEALING

Dear DONM,

I wanted to talk to you today about freewriting.

Freewriting is just what it says—writing freely. It is a terrific tool for all sorts of purposes: for getting in touch with your subconscious to know what's really going on for you, for accessing buried emotions and processing them and moving on from them, and for increasing creativity.

What you do with freewriting is this: you put pen to paper and you write, without stopping, for a set length of time or a set number of pages. It is important that you put pen to paper rather than use the computer, as freewriting is a very kinesthetic process; it's about being in your body and using your body, and physical handwriting facilitates that much more than typing on a computer. I recommend a pen rather than pencil for ease of writing quickly, and I have even experimented with different pens to find the smoothest ones.

When you start this, your hand can get tired, but just persevere; your hand will get stronger soon.

The most important aspect to freewriting is this: write quickly, without stopping, and do not worry about the quality. It does not matter what you write, only that you do write. By freeing yourself from worrying about what you write, you switch off the internal critic, and that is hugely freeing, especially for DONMs who have been so accustomed to constant criticism.

When you freewrite, you are responsible for the quantity (the agreed amount of time or pages), but you bear no responsibility for the quality. Do not fret over the words you use, or your spelling, or your grammar, or the quality of your handwriting. Your success comes from doing it, not from how it is done.

There are various ways you can incorporate freewriting in your life. One of the most famous is what's called Morning Pages (made famous by Julia Cameron in her excellent book *The Artist's Way*). You keep a notebook and pen beside your bed, and as soon as you wake up in the morning, while your mind is still half-asleep, before your inner critic has time to wake up, you write three pages. (You can go to the toilet first if you need to, of course! But apart from that, the ideal is to do this before you get up or have coffee or do any other morning routines.)

The three pages should be fairly big—A4 in Europe or the equivalent (approximately 8.5 x 11 in.) in America. This is important, as I will explain in a minute.

So, what do you write? Anything. Again, don't judge it. I often start off with a comment on the weather that I see through the window. I write about how I feel physically—still tired, or refreshed, any aches I have, etc. I might write about what happened yesterday, or my hopes for today. A lot of it, frankly, is hugely banal stuff, but that's okay!

The essential thing is to keep the hand moving. In a way, if you commit to keeping the pen moving, the writing happens *through* you and not *by* you. The words come, and if they don't, just write that fact, like this: "I don't know what to write next, not sure what to say now, no idea what to write . . ."

If I filled three pages with that, it would still be good because I would still have done the exercise. But in practice, what happens is that the brain gets bored with writing like that, and after two or three lines, I'll find I'm writing something more solid. When I say "I find I'm writing," that's exactly what it's like: I don't think what to write and then write it. I write and see what comes flowing out of the pen.

I can tend to be somewhat ADD, and doing three pages in one go was tough at the start. But that was okay—I just wrote my frustration at it: "I resent doing this. I'm so bored now. This is ridiculous. Why am I doing this? I wonder what happened on my favorite websites overnight . . ." But even as I'm writing that, it means I'm still writing and so still doing it correctly.

Three pages is the magic number because that is long enough to let the top layer of crud out of your brain and begin to get into deeper layers underneath. This doesn't happen immediately; I have frequently written three pages of extremely banal drivel, with no insights coming at all. When insights do come, they come on the third page.

I see patterns. I find I'm writing about the same topic over and over, revisiting it without realizing why. But I therefore realize that this topic is obviously important to me.

I have toyed with freewriting many times before, but about six weeks ago I committed to it. And there have been huge shifts in my life since, for the better. Coincidence? Perhaps. I think not, though.

Even without the shifts, even if they were coincidental, I'd find it hugely rewarding to do. The first thing is that I can guarantee that I will start every day with a success. That is so empowering and really sets me up for the day. Beyond that, freewriting gives me insights into what's going on for me. Amid the banality and whining, there are gems of awareness that really make sense to me and help me. So I do recommend it strongly.

Another way to use freewriting is if you have a problem or a decision to make, freewrite about that. Say you are debating taking a job or moving to another city or a big decision like that. You could set the timer for, say, fifteen minutes and just start writing your thoughts about the dilemma.

Or write your pain and upset at an incident, either recent or in the past. In this way you're using freewriting to process your emotions and let them go. As we discussed before, emotions cannot hurt you, so do not be scared of this.

As a DONM, you can use freewriting to explore how you feel about all that happened to you. You can write a letter to a younger you, or a letter from a younger you. You can write to your narcissistic mother and say all you want to say. (Without sending it, of course. This is for you.)

Freewriting is a hugely powerful tool, and I invite you to use it.

Hugs,
Danu

YOUR GRIEF AND BEREAVEMENT

Dear DONM,

Once you have truly accepted that your narcissistic mother has never loved you, can never love you, and will never love you, a number of things will happen.

The first is that, as explained previously, you will finally be free of banging your head against the wall, of flying constantly into the window. Free of trying to achieve the impossible. That is the good news.

However, there is a downside to it, in that you may well experience deep sadness and grief. This makes perfect sense when you think about it—you absolutely have suffered a huge loss, a massive bereavement.

You have, in a very real sense, lost your mother, just as much as if she had died. You are experiencing the death of the image of the loving, kind, decent, supportive mother you hoped and even believed she would one day become. That is truly a loss that is not to be underestimated.

This grief is made worse, I believe, because it's such a private grief. In the case of a real death, society supports us in our grieving: people understand what we're going through, and our friends rally around, and there is a cultural framework in the form of a funeral to help us through this grief.

In the case of letting go of the hope that our mother will ever change, there is no such help. Unless we're very lucky, even our spouses and close friends won't understand.

As for getting through the grief, just know that, as with all grief, time itself will help with that, at least to some extent.

Here are a few steps to help you process it, though.

First, don't underestimate the enormity of what you're going through. Be gentle with yourself at this time. Understand that you might feel weepy and upset just as if you had experienced a literal bereavement. I suggest you honor this and don't dismiss it, and above all, don't beat yourself up for it.

If at all possible, enroll the help of friends or your spouse or partner. They probably will not understand, but if they choose to, they can help even without understanding. If they simply take your word for it that this is, for you, like it would be for them if their loving mother died, then they can offer the same support they would like to have in that circumstance.

Freewriting will help you to work through the grief. Another option to help with the grief is EFT. EFT is really good for processing emotions, and the emotion of grief is no different. You can just tap the points as you're feeling the sadness and grief.

The most important thing is to know that this grief will pass, that it will ease, and that joy and peace are waiting for you.

Hugs,
Danu

THE TRAUMA YOU SUFFERED

Dear DONM,

Could you be suffering from post-traumatic stress disorder (PTSD)?

Nonsense, you might say. That's only for those who experienced a war zone, or some other similarly intense tragedy.

The thing is, in many ways, being raised in a narcissistic household is like being in a war zone. The constant stress and fear are very similar.

What you might have is complex PTSD, or C-PTSD. Wikipedia describes it like this:

> Complex post-traumatic stress disorder (C-PTSD) is a psychological injury that results from protracted exposure to prolonged social and/or interpersonal trauma in the context of either captivity or entrapment (i.e., the lack of a viable escape route for the victim) that results in the lack or loss of control, helplessness, and deformations of identity and sense of self.
>
> Forms of trauma associated with C-PTSD include sexual abuse (especially child sexual abuse), physical abuse, emotional abuse, domestic violence or torture—all repeated traumas in which there is an actual or perceived inability for the victim to escape.

Doesn't that sound exactly like our situation?

EFT is superb for clearing trauma and even erasing it. Work either with an EFT practitioner or by yourself, which is very doable. If you don't wish to use EFT, do consider getting yourself good therapy to work through the trauma. Or both, of course: EFT and therapy.

Don't underestimate what you experienced, and do claim all the resources you need to heal it.

Hugs,
Danu

WHAT ABOUT TELLING SIBLINGS?

Dear DONM,

There can be a big temptation, when you find out the truth about your mother's narcissism, to want to share it with siblings and others.

That's totally understandable. You feel that you are free, now that you know the truth, or freer at least, and you want to help them be free too. They might even be allies with you in dealing with your mother. It'll be great!

But hold up.

This can be a tricky one to maneuver. It's a big step, and not one that is to be taken lightly. It can very easily backfire on you. Your siblings may well have a very different relationship with your mother than you do. They might be the favorite child who can do no wrong (known as the "golden child"), while you are the one who can never do right (the "scapegoat"). Their relationship with her might be working well for them, albeit in a dysfunctional codependent way. They most likely will not want that disturbed.

Even if their relationship with her is fraught, they may not be ready to hear the truth. As you have possibly experienced yourself, it's hugely upsetting to learn that your own mother does not love you, that she cannot love you, and that she will not love you ever. It demands a whole reevaluation of your life, your self, everything. Your sibling might not be in a place to hear it.

Not able to hear it, needing to defend themselves from this unwelcome news, they might react badly. Aggressively, even. They might perceive it as an attack—which it is, really—an attack on their current reality, no matter how helpfully you mean it or how kindly you say it.

As attacked people tend to do, they will defend themselves in any way possible. They could turn on you, asking how you dare say such horrible, nasty things about your lovely, sainted mother. They may refuse to talk to you, cutting off contact either temporarily or permanently. They may even go back and tell your mother what you're saying about her—and the stuff will really hit the fan then.

So, that's it then? You've no choice but to leave them wallowing in the pain, dysfunction, and abuse? You've escaped from it, but they have to keep enduring it?

That, of course, is the dilemma.

You do have a choice as to whether to tell them or not. You have to make that choice, and there is no single right answer.

You know them best. They might be delighted to hear the news. It might feel like the key to the prison gates.

But, as described above, they might not. How do you know which it will be?

The trick, I think, is to start with small questions. If you're used to venting at each other about her, maybe say something like, "Why do you think she's like this?" and see what they say, if they're up for exploring the topic.

If you've never spoken before about her behavior, start with that— "Does it annoy you when she does x?"—and see how responsive your sibling is to discussing it. Watch out for signs of your sibling closing up or getting defensive, and back off immediately if that happens.

If they seem receptive, ask another small question, or make a small observation and see how that goes.

If your sibling isn't ready to hear this, then you need to respect that. It's horrible to see them still suffering when you know the answer, but truly, you can't do anything about that. You can stay alert for signs that they might be shifting in their openness as time passes and test them every so often on their willingness by using another small question.

Hugs,
Danu

NORMAL RULES DON'T APPLY
WITH NARCISSISTS

Dear DONM,

One of the biggest weapons narcissists use against us is our manners. They put us in no-win situations where our niceness and our decency and our social awareness work against us.

Classic example: We're not talking to them. We don't want to talk to them. We might even have gone "no contact" (NC), which means to formally sever all contact between them and us. We might even have informed them that we are NC and that they are not to contact us.

But say a gift from her arrives in the mail for us or for a member of our family. It would be so rude to not acknowledge that, so we need to send a thank-you letter. In this way we fall into her trap of contacting her again.

However, the good news is that no, we don't have to thank her! We don't have to fall into any trap. Here's the thing:

With narcissists, the normal rules don't apply. That might seem quite radical, but it's really good news. They break all the rules of social interaction and human cooperation, after all, and therefore, we are not bound to those rules when we're dealing with them.

I repeat, they have broken the rules of society already. They consistently do this. You are at a serious disadvantage if you keep playing by those rules, which is, of course, what they are counting on.

Can you imagine playing, say, golf with somebody who wouldn't play by the rules? Instead of playing the ball as it lay, your opponent would pick it up each time and put it in a position favorable to herself, to allow for easy putting, or maybe even just pick it up and drop it in the hole.

You, on the other hand, scrupulously keep to the rules. You are not going to start cheating when it's your turn. This is partly because of the narcissist's web of confusion: the cheating is so subtle you don't notice it, or it's so blatant you can't believe it and therefore discount it as something you imagined.

The other reason you don't cheat is because you're a decent, kind person who wants to play by the rules.

Now, between you and her, who is going to win that golf game? And every future game? And by what huge margin?

The only recourse is to either stop playing (and we'll be talking about that soon) or to cheat in turn.

But *cheat* is an emotive term, and my analogy falls apart there. Because it's not cheating. It's recognizing that what you're playing is not golf, no matter how much you thought it was golf, no matter how often she tells you it's golf, and no matter how much you want to keep to the rules of golf.

You're playing a different game, with different rules and, in many ways, with no rules at all. It's fine for you to break the rules of golf when it's not golf you're playing.

I know it goes against the grain and can seem shocking to do, but once you get the hang of it, it is very liberating. You don't have to thank her for gifts (such gifts really just being drama-fodder and manipulation anyway and not genuine gifts). You don't have to send her birthday cards or other cards. You don't have to include her in your family celebrations. (I had both my fortieth birthday party and a book launch without inviting my parents, and it was the best decision both times.) You don't have to return her phone calls, texts, or emails. You don't have to "friend" her on Facebook or respond to her statuses if she is a friend.

The only rule you need to worry about is the rule to protect yourself and your family from her manipulation.

So I suggest you watch out for the times she tries to manipulate you into doing things because it's the polite thing to do—and refuse to fall for it.

Normal rules don't apply with narcissists. That's half their power; they don't play by the rules, while knowing we will. We regain our power by realizing that, when it comes to dealing with them, the rules don't apply to us either.

Hugs,
Danu

INTRODUCING RULE 1

Dear DONM,

One of the things I noticed again and again when I was running the forum for DONMs was that women would often ask us what they should do in a specific circumstance. It really wasn't our place to tell them what to do, but I totally understood why they were asking: their narcissistic mothers had them so confused that half the time they didn't realize what they *could* do, what they should do, what they were allowed to do, and so on.

So we introduced a rule simply called Rule 1: Do what you want to do. (Fittingly, we also had Rule 2, which was: If in doubt, refer to Rule 1.)

It was often somewhat mind-blowing for these women to be told this amazing concept. Not surprisingly, it had never occurred to them before that they could do what they wanted to do when their narcissistic mother had spent a lifetime telling them they had to do what *she* wanted them to do.

We DONMs were taught so much, so hard, so long, and so convincingly that our needs, wants, and desires did not matter at all, that it is very difficult for us to realize that they do matter.

Our needs, wants, and desires matter greatly. This can be a whole new mindset.

The first thing to accept is the concept itself: that it's okay to want your own way sometimes; to know that sometimes it is about you and that what is important is what you want, rather than what anyone else wants.

Let that sink in for a moment. Think about it.

Does it feel scary? Does it feel enormous and threatening? The very idea that it should be about what you want can seem very scary indeed when you are not used to that.

But, in your new life of freedom—or as we in the forum called it, freeDONM—this is essential to learn: it is important that you do what you want to do.

Now, of course we're not talking about being inappropriately selfish or self-centered or neglecting your responsibilities or anything like that. If you have children, then for sure it is essential to meet their needs before your own desires. (Indeed, meeting your own desires before your children's needs is a quintessentially narcissistic thing to do.)

Likewise, if you have a job or a business or other responsibilities, then of course you have to see to those and honor those.

But outside that kind of responsibility, truly, what you want is important and should be given very high priority when you're making decisions about what you're going to do or not do. So, the answer to any dilemma you might have is: do what you want to do.

If it is your birthday and your mother wants you to spend it with her but you were dreading the idea, then you need only ask yourself, "What do I want to do?"

If you were dreading spending the day with her, then it is very clear that you do not want to do this. So, based on Rule 1, which is to do what you want to do, you do not spend the day with her. Instead you choose to spend your birthday in a way that supports you and is enjoyable for you.

Will there be repercussions? Yes, of course there will be. She will not be happy about this at all. She will even complain, or undergo narcissistic rage (which is like a temper tantrum for narcissists). We'll discuss soon how to deal with her narcissistic rage.

For now, just start thinking about what you would like to do. Even if you're not in a position to actually do it yet, it's good to get the practice in even identifying what you want to do.

As ever, you can use EFT to help you identify this if you're not sure about it. Just tap, using the statement "Even though I don't even know what I want to do, I love and accept myself anyway," and use the rest of the process after that. In a very short time, your actual real desires will bubble up and you will be very clear about what you want to do.

Hugs,
Danu

DEALING WITH THE SHAME

Dear DONM,

The writer John Bradshaw called it "toxic shame." It's not normal healthy shame that comes when we do something wrong and that helps us behave well. Rather, toxic shame is the shame we carry to our very core about who we are.

It's not surprising that DONMs have a lot of that. We were taught to be deeply ashamed of ourselves. We were taught that we were flawed, shameful, born broken. We had to be seen as damaged so she could be seen (by herself at least, but also by others) as perfect. We took that and carried it because we knew no better. And we carry it still.

We feel that we are innately broken and damaged and grotesque. That if others knew this truth about us, they'd never want anything to do with us. As a result, we're always hiding ourselves, portraying what feels like a false self, and so feeling (and in one way, being) inauthentic as we hide what we think is our true self.

The irony, of course, is that we are not the shameful, twisted, distorted self she told us we were, and that therefore the false self we show the world is nearer to our real self than the self we think we are. Does that make sense?

What I mean is that we think we are hiding a nonexistent nasty self and portraying a nice real self, but we are the only one who doesn't realize what's actually happening. Our friends and family see the real, true nice self. But we twist ourselves in knots hiding this big, shameful secret, when in fact there is no secret to hide at all.

Who we are is an ordinary, nice, decent human being with an average set of flaws.

Now, to digress a bit, of course the self we show is false to an extent. As the poet T. S. Eliot put it, we put on a face to meet the faces that we meet. But I don't think it's false as such. We put on clothes to meet all but our closest intimates, and we put on metaphorical clothes for different situations.

But that just means there are different roles for different relationships, different levels of exposure. The face we show to the world is just a dressed, polished, expression of ourselves. It's still us, just as a dressed me is still me.

So that digression was to show that the public face we have is no lie—just a clothed version of the real self.

To get back to my main point, when we think of shame, is it possible to just know that we do not have to be ashamed? That we are okay just as we are. That our narcissistic mother's lies were layered onto us, wrapped around us, trying to force us into the shape of a gargoyle.

We can reject that. We can hand back that false shame.

One way is by recognizing the shame when we feel it, and proactively giving ourselves a different message.

That might not be easy, though, as the shame is so subtle, so insidious. It flashes through our awareness more quickly than we can tell, leaving just its scar.

But with practice and diligence it is possible.

I, of course, suggest that tapping/EFT is the way to deal with the shame the easy way, so I invite you to try that.

Hugs,
Danu

BOUNDARIES ARE YOUR
GREATEST GIFT TO YOURSELF

Dear DONM,

I spoke of boundaries in my book *You're Not Crazy*, but they're so important that I want to go into more detail about them here.

You are entitled to set your boundaries where you please, no matter if others think they're unreasonable. Indeed, you're entitled to them, even if they *are* unreasonable (to exaggerate the point for emphasis). If you said, for example, that people could only phone you between the hours of 2:00 and 2:30 each day, that would be your right. Of course, others have the right to find that boundary unreasonable and to not call you at all. But they don't have the right to call at other times when you've stated that it's not acceptable.

How much more does that truth apply if you are setting reasonable boundaries?

Boundaries are your birthright, and you are entitled to them. Setting boundaries is telling the world—and more importantly, yourself—that you have value. That you are not their chew-toy. That you claim your own space, both literally and metaphorically.

I offer you the possibility of creating your own personal manifesto regarding your boundaries. Think about them, and then write them down. Writing things down has impact and power far beyond merely thinking of something.

It can be hard for DONMs to even think what their boundaries might be, as we have been so trained to not even consider our own boundaries—or even the possibility of having them.

One suggestion is to think of what annoys you when it happens: that's a clue that one of your boundaries is being breached. For example, if it really annoys you when your friend talks at you on the phone for hours, then a reasonable and legitimate boundary might be that you will not speak on the phone for more than half an hour. Or that she has to check whether or not it's a good time for you before she starts talking and accept it gracefully if it's not.

Here is a list of possible boundaries—a menu for you from which to pick and choose—but please be clear that this is just to spark your imagination so you can think of your own.

- No one is allowed to just come over to my house without phoning first.

- No one is allowed to let themselves into my house.

- Once in my house, no one is allowed to root around in the cupboards.

- No one is allowed to touch me without my permission.

- No one is allowed to comment adversely on my weight/appearance/state of my house.

- I have the right to say, "I'll think about it and get back to you," rather than being pressured into things.

- I have the right to change my mind.

- I have the right to say no without further explanation.

- I have the right to not answer the phone if it does not suit me.

- I have the right to refuse to answer personal questions.

- I have the right to put limits on visits: "You may stop over between 2:00 and 4:00."

Now, of course sometimes you will relax those boundaries. Spouses and children are allowed to touch you, for example. They're still keeping to the boundary, though, as they already have permission. And I know that with my close friends, I'm quite entitled to go to the kitchen to make tea myself, as they are in my house. But again, I/they are doing this with permission. The difference is that you lower the boundaries as per your choice, not have them knocked down by someone else's disregard for them.

One thing about boundaries is that you get to say what is not allowed to happen, but you are not allowed to say what *will* happen. So you can say, "You can only phone between 2:00 and 2:30" (i.e., they cannot phone outside those times, in effect), but you cannot say, "You must phone me then." That would be imposing on the other person's freedoms. (This, funnily enough, is something narcissistic mothers themselves fail to grasp.)

In the next letter we'll discuss how to enforce and keep these boundaries, which is not at all easy with a narcissist.

Hugs,
Danu

MORE ABOUT BOUNDARIES

Dear DONM,

The thing is, narcissists hate boundaries. They hate them with a passion. They feel attacked by them. How *dare* you tell them what they can and can't do? That's an absolute assault. They feel justified in reacting with major force. They'll do whatever they need to do in order to knock that boundary down. They might rage at you until you remove the boundary, or they might just ignore the boundary and dare you to challenge them. (And woe to you if you do challenge them. Cue narcissistic rage.)

So what do you do?

One option is to let them get away with it. To never have boundaries with them. To let them come over whenever they like, phone whenever they like, ask you any questions they want, no matter how personal—and you answer them too! That is definitely the easier option. That'll keep the peace for you.

But at what cost?

The cost of your own self-esteem. Your own space. Your own authority to make your own decisions about your own life. Your own privacy. Your own thoughts. Your autonomy.

All of those things are valuable, and it will cost you those to keep the peace. If you are prepared for that price, then it's fine. Please understand that I have no opinion about what you do in this case, no attachment to you taking any particular path. I'm simply attempting to lay out the options and the pros and cons of each.

So, yes, keep going as you always have been, if that is your choice, and know the price you are paying. It may well be worth it, and I mean that genuinely, not as snide sarcasm.

The other option is to start putting boundaries in place, such as the ones on the list you may have written. In each case, create a consequence for her breaking the boundary. It needs to be a consequence that's in your power to enact. Leaving her presence and/or hanging up the phone are good ones.

In each case the magic trick is to carry out the consequence regardless of how she tries to wriggle out of it. Here is an example:

You state the boundary calmly. If the boundary continues to be broken, you tell her the consequences of breaking it. You either do it ahead of time ("Mom, I am not happy with you always going on about my weight, and I'm asking you now to stop doing that whenever we meet.") or you do it in the moment, the next time she mentions your weight.

She may huff and puff and invalidate in one of the many ways narcissists have: "Oh, you're ridiculous, I am only trying to *help*," or "You can't take a joke!" or something along those lines.

She may cry and sob (especially if the other tricks don't work), "Oh, you're so mean, it's not fair," etc., etc.

Whatever she says, you ignore it. You don't get caught up in a discussion about it (because your boundaries are not open for discussion, especially not discussion aimed at derailing). You just say calmly, "That may be so, but the fact remains that I am asking you now to stop mentioning my weight." Or, if she's crying, "I'm sorry you're upset, but the fact remains that I'm asking you now to stop mentioning my weight."

If she continues mentioning your weight regardless, you tell her the consequence: "Mom, I am asking you to stop talking about my weight. If you do not, I will leave/hang up whenever you talk about it."

Likewise, if she escalates to an argument, you say, "Mom, I'm going to have to ask you to stop shouting at me, or I will have to leave/hang up/ask you to leave."

Then, when she continues, as she most likely will, you do exactly what you said: you leave/hang up, etc. And the next time, you do it again.

What you are doing is literally training her, like we train a dog, with consequences. She doesn't have to like it—in fact, it's guaranteed that she won't. But that's okay. If one of you has to be unhappy, it doesn't have to be you.

Your narcissistic mother will fight and scream and object, make no mistake. She will fight this with everything she's got. To her, this boundary, which thwarts her desire, feels like an attack, like the end of the world in a way I don't think normal people can really understand.

Her upset will be the greatest the first few times you do this. It's like disciplining a spoiled child or an untrained puppy—they won't like the new regimen and will fight it and challenge it every way they can, until they learn that you mean it and won't give in to their tactics. This is why it's essential to stay strong and consistent when you do this.

Two things about all of this: First, she will learn, regardless, once you are consistent about enforcing the consequences. Second, in truth, "everything she's got" isn't much, when it comes down to it. It's upset and bluster and rage. It's noise and fury, is all. (Unless, of course, she's physically violent and/or controls you financially, in which case none of this advice about boundaries applies and you need to sort it out as you would with any violent person.)

I know that this is all scary stuff. The prospect of standing up to your mother when she bullied you all your life can be overwhelming. As ever, I recommend EFT to help you deal with that fear.

One last thing to note: most likely, she'll constantly push the boundary, trying to get you to drop it, or trying to cheat. She might mention a celebrity who's put on a lot of weight and give you a sly look, daring you to react to that. If she gets away with that, then she'll try something a bit closer to home and see how far she can push it. It is exhausting, but you will have to keep enforcing the boundaries, or go back to square one. Ahhh, the joys of dealing with a narcissist.

It's also very possible she'll go into full-blown narcissistic rage. We talk about that next.

Hugs,
Danu

DEALING WITH NARCISSISTIC RAGE

Dear DONM,

Narcissistic rage is the absolute temper that narcissists get into when they have been thwarted or otherwise upset. Given that a narcissist is really just a small child in an adult body, we can truly and accurately call these "tantrums."

That's all they are, you know, the same tantrums that toddlers have. But whereas we are able to deal with the child's tantrum—well, even that can be difficult sometimes—it is much harder to deal with the tantrum of the narcissistic mother.

This is because we have been sensitized all our life to be scared of her. We have been trained to fear her rage. Even though we are adults now, when she starts in on this rage, we still go to the flight-or-fight response. Our body tenses, our stomach churns, our throat gets dry: in short, all the symptoms of extreme stress. This is called the flight-or-fight response, but one of the other responses in that pattern is to freeze, and that's what usually happens to us. We learned early on that we could not fight, and as a child we could not flee, so our learned response is to freeze.

Not surprisingly, we will do anything we can to avoid this horrible experience. This is why so many of us tend to put up with such bad behavior from our narcissistic mothers, which is why, even if we know what we want to do, we often don't do it. To continue the example when I spoke of Rule 1, we may well know that we do not want to spend our birthday with her, but it is just too difficult to face up to the rage and upset that she will inflict upon us if we choose that option.

So, how to deal with it?

When you feel the panic and stress, remind yourself that this is an old pattern. That it is based on beliefs about what she can do to you. Yes, it is true that when you were a child, her anger was very dangerous to you as she really could inflict damage on you or, even if she never did, that possibility was always there. As children we are dependent upon our parents for our very survival, so her anger at us was a very real, if primal, threat to our safety.

Now that we are adults, there is nothing, really, that she can do to us.

Now, before I continue in this vein, I need to stress that most narcissistic mothers are not physically violent. Physical violence is not a trait of narcissists as such. It is much more a trait of sociopaths and psychopaths. Having said that, if your mother is likely to be violent and to inflict real damage on you, then of course this advice does not apply. You need to take all reasonable steps to defend yourself from physical attack.

Also, if you are in a horrible situation such as your financial well-being depending on her (and narcissistic mothers are very good at contriving such situations), then you might be best not to antagonize her.

But if the violence is "only" verbal and psychological and emotional, which is the normal narcissistic way, and if you are not dependent on her, then the following should be possible: when she starts her rage, just try to step aside a little bit from your emotions about it.

Don't try to deny your emotions—this is essential. You are really feeling them, and it is important to validate that. Nothing I'm telling you is about you invalidating what is going on for you; your mother did enough invalidating all your life, and a large part of the healing journey is that you *do* validate what is going on for you and acknowledge it.

So do not deny the fear you're feeling, the stress you're feeling. But try to step a little bit aside from it and observe it, and in that way, it will lose some of its power.

Also try to observe your mother's behavior from an emotional distance. (A physical distance would be great too, but that might not be possible.) Try to see her rage as the tantrum it is. Observe it as being so pathetic and ridiculous, as it really is. I mean, really, a grown woman throwing a hissy fit because her daughter won't do something small that she wanted her to do! This is ridiculous by any standard.

Try to observe, try to be objective, and in this way, her rage will lose a lot of its power over you. Perhaps even observe it as if you were an anthropologist observing a different culture, in the sense that you are clear and present and observing it, but you are not involved in it.

The thing is, though, no matter how much you recognize all this on a logical, rational basis, your *body* doesn't know that. You know it's true, but you don't *feel* that it's true.

And so, as ever, I offer you EFT. EFT will change your feelings about this at a core level so that you feel calm and detached whenever she throws a tantrum. You can use EFT when you are on your own, to build up your resistance to her rage.

I repeat, you were programmed to fear her. But it does not have to stay like that.

Next, I'll share some hints and tips for how to react when she's in narcissistic rage.

Hugs,
Danu

WHEN SHE'S IN FULL-BLOWN
NARCISSISTIC RAGE

Dear DONM,

We're going to explore some ideas of what to say to your mother in the moment when she's in a rage. Note that these are only ideas, that you know your own mother best, and that you always need to be mindful of your own safety. That said, here are some suggestions:

You're probably stuck doing things you've already agreed to do, but this is for new arrangements. Let's say she says happily, "Oh, your birthday's soon! What'll we do for it? I always wanted to go to x place; let's do that!" How do you deal with that?

The motto "Never explain; never apologize" is a good one here. You can by all means say "sorry" as a conversational gesture, but don't genuinely apologize, as you aren't doing anything wrong. And don't explain (i.e., give reasons/make excuses) because she'll no doubt erode whatever explanation you give. So, "I can't spend my birthday with you because I promised Jane I'd spend it with her" will get you:

"But Jane doesn't love you as much as I do, and what did she do for you that I didn't, and that's so unfair, because you spent x other occasion with Jane, and Jane always comes before me," etc.

So if at all possible, just say casually, "I'm afraid I won't be able to spend my birthday with you. But maybe we can meet the following Saturday to celebrate it if you like"—if you're happy to give her a consolation prize. If not, don't say anything about that bit. Just try to change the subject to talking about her: "I'm afraid I won't be able to spend my birthday with you after all. Oh, did you get a new dress? It's beautiful on you!"

It's possible she'll be diverted, just as a toddler can be, especially as your new topic of conversation is about her.

But it's equally possible she won't be.

If she says, "Why not?" just say calmly, "I have other plans"—and try again to change the subject. If she persists, maybe try using a technique out of the brilliant book *How to Talk So Kids Will Listen, and Listen So Kids Will Talk*. It's about how to parent well, as you'd guess from the title. And since our narcissistic mothers are children at heart, many of the techniques in this book can be tried with them.

The one I'm suggesting here is to reflect their feelings back to them. Say something like, "I can see you're very upset. I can imagine you're very frustrated and hurt by this."

And she might snap, "Yes, I am! That my own daughter won't spend her birthday with me! The anniversary of the day, let me remind you, that I spent thirteen hours in labor, in agony!"

Don't engage in her specific points, because that way lies defeat. Just say something like, "Yes, I can see you're very hurt, all right"—not patronizingly, but genuinely. This is a means of reflecting her emotions back to her. Validating them, really. Her emotions are very real to her, no matter how unjustified they are. (And, in fact, I suspect that narcissists, like toddlers, feel things even more strongly than the rest of us as they have no control over their emotions.)

So, real and true validation is a very powerful thing. You can say things like, "I'm sorry that you're feeling so upset." This might sound like a contradiction of what I said above, to never apologize, but it's not really. An apology would be to concede that she has more right over your birthday plans than you do and that, therefore, you're wrong to claim those rights for yourself. If you say, "I'm sorry

I can't be with you on my birthday," that would be an apology. But "I'm sorry you're upset" is using the other meaning of "I'm sorry," the one that means more "I'm sad about the fact that . . ."

So, what I'm saying is: don't be sucked into discussing your decision to spend your birthday elsewhere, but do try to comfort her about her upset without taking responsibility for it.

If she refuses to calm down, then you might consider saying calmly, "I am sorry that you are upset. It's clear that I'm upsetting you more. I'll leave/hang up now and let you gather yourself. Give me a call when you feel up to talking about it calmly." This last sentence is important as you're clearly leaving the ball in her court.

I know this sounds almost blasphemous. For sure it's changing the whole pattern of your encounters. But either the dynamic changes or everything stays the same and you remain under her thumb, which, honestly, is a fully valid option.

You understand that I am not advocating rebellion? That would not be my place at all. Sometimes the path of least resistance is the right one. You might not be in a position to stand up to her and change the dynamic. And that's quite all right.

But if you are in a position to change the dynamic, and you're tired of living your life as her chew-toy, and you want to incorporate Rule 1 ("Do what you want to do") in your life . . . well, then, by definition, your behavior has to change. Her behavior surely won't—why would it, when up until now it has gotten her all she wants?

True, she won't like it. But that's okay. Remember: if one of you has to be upset, it doesn't have to be you.

As I said earlier, her upset will be the greatest the first few times you do this, until she learns better.

Be prepared for tantrums—just deal with those as suggested above.

Be aware that she might stop talking to you to try to guilt you into crawling back to her. That often works. Their silence is very powerful for as long as we let it be. But if you can see it as the manipulation it is, then you have the choice of letting it continue. See who blinks first. It's very likely that she will crack first, when her need for your attention becomes stronger than her need to ignore you.

Most likely she'll contact you most cheerfully, with no reference to all that went before, as if you had parted in great form only a day or two previously. It's probably best, especially if you got your way, to play along with that and just carry on.

None of it is easy. I know that. But it is doable, and in that lies your power.

Hugs,
Danu

WHAT IF SHE CRIES?

Dear DONM,

If rage doesn't work, she might well turn to tears. This was certainly my own mother's tactic, and I know she's not alone. If she can't gain your fear, she may well make a play for your sympathy. She might sob something like, "Oh, it's so unfair! You always hurt me. After all I've done for you. It hurts so much that my own daughter doesn't want to spend her birthday with me," etc.

What do you do then? In many ways this is harder to deal with than her rage. You feel like such a monster. You feel so guilty and horrible; you must be a bad, awful, nasty person to upset your mother like this. She was right with everything she said about you, wasn't she?

The thing is, though, that this is just pure manipulation. She wants her way, and she'll do everything she can to get it. I don't deny that there's genuine emotion in there too, as she has been thwarted in getting what she wants and is genuinely upset about that. But it's all designed to make you cave in to her wishes.

I know the pull is very strong when she does this—the need or desire to placate her, to calm her, to make the tears stop. You might well give in to her. It's okay if you do. Don't beat yourself up about it. She has been playing this game a long time, and she's very good at it. It's totally understandable that you would concede.

But maybe think ahead of time what you might do in the case of tears, and come up with a plan. You might choose to know that disappointment comes to us all, and that it's not your job to protect her from that. You might choose to know that she is choosing this upset, or certainly the scale of it, and that that's up to her and is not your responsibility. You might choose to be strong, and even firm, in support of your own wishes, needs, and desires. You are fully entitled to do this as long as your original choice was an ethical and fair one, which I'm sure it was. You wouldn't expect to celebrate your birthday instead of supporting her through a major operation, I bet. In these examples we're talking about honoring your wishes above her whims.

You could choose to comfort her for her genuine upset and call her bluff, in a way, for her manipulative upset. You could honor her tears without conceding to her desires. "I'm sorry you're upset, Mom," you might say. "I can see you're disappointed." But if she sobs something like, "I'd stop crying if only you agreed to do what I want," or hints at that—well, you can remain kind and strong at the same time. Witness her tears and comfort her without giving in to them. It is the same as if you had a child crying because she couldn't have chocolate for dinner; you could empathize and comfort her about her upset, but you wouldn't even consider giving in to what she wanted because it would not be right. The same applies here.

Hugs,
Danu

THE SILENT TREATMENT

Dear DONM,

Narcissistic rage is one tactic, and tears is another, and yet another is to ignore you. To sulk, basically. To effectively banish you from her presence until you cave and give in to her.

Especially if you say kindly and calmly, "I'll leave now; get back in touch when you're able to discuss it calmly." Well, she might not get in touch at all.

This is a surprisingly powerful action. None of us likes to be banished. None of us wants to live in that limbo where she's not talking to us, where she's angry with us. The silence can be portrayed by her and/or understood by us to be because she is so hurt at our sheer cruelty to her, and we hate making her so miserable.

So, this tactic often works to bring us to heel. To have us calling and apologizing even though we did nothing wrong. To do whatever it takes to get back into her good graces, no matter the cost to our own autonomy and our own self-esteem, or to do whatever it takes to stop her pain, no matter how much it is self-inflicted.

But the thing is, her silent treatment is an empty gesture on her behalf. It only has the impact and value and weight we give it. She's banking on that. We can choose to either ignore the impact it has on us or to erase the impact it has on us.

To ignore it, you can feel the fear and stress and upset of it all, just as you always did when this has happened before. But you allow those feelings to be felt fully, without judgment, without resistance. Allow them to turn up, to live for a while in your body. It's uncomfortable, but it's not dangerous in any way. A lot of the discomfort about it comes from our resistance to the feelings, from our fear about experiencing them, but when we allow them, the resistance and fear are neutralized. As the feelings are allowed to present themselves, they'll fade and disappear.

Just feel the feelings without believing you have to act upon them. You can feel dreadful about the fact that she's angry with you or hurting badly, without taking the step (which is nothing less than your complete surrender, don't forget) to stop her from being angry with you or hurt.

You'll have to keep doing this. The feelings will often come back with every thought about her—every time the phone rings and it's not her, for example. But each time, you can feel the feelings calmly and they will go.

Rather than just ignoring the feelings, you can erase them using EFT. You can tap whenever you feel the stress and fear, tapping while breathing deeply, until it passes.

The whole situation isn't easy, I know, but you are fighting for nothing less than your own autonomy, don't forget. You are fighting for the right to say no to her, to make your own decisions. This is a battle worth fighting, I think. This one will be the hardest, as you're changing the rules and she, of course, is resisting it.

So, a battle worth fighting. Your weapon is . . . to do nothing. Doing nothing might seem like a very passive thing, but in the right situation it is an extremely powerfully proactive action.

You carefully left the ball in her court, so it's up to her to contact you.

Now, you need to know that it's possible that she will never contact you again. It's possible that her anger at your insubordination, or her love of the drama of haranguing about your cruelty, or her indifference, might lead her to cut you off completely. You need to think about this and see if you're okay with that outcome. It's a big decision for sure, and I don't seek to influence it. I do throw out this question, however: If someone's presence in your life is wholly dependent upon you obeying them fully, how healthy a relationship is that?

However, it's unlikely she'll let you go. (I mean "unlikely" in the sense of what most narcissistic mothers would do, so statistically unlikely. Obviously I don't know your mother or how she'll react, so I can't predict that.) If she's like most narcissistic mothers, she needs you as her source of narcissistic supply. (*Narcissistic supply* is the name given to narcissists' addiction to attention.) It's most likely, therefore, that she'll do the silent treatment to bring you to heel, and when she realizes it isn't working and/or her need for your attention trumps her need to punish you, then she will contact you.

In my own mother's case, it took nine months.

My situation was slightly different in that I knew I didn't want to see her again, and so the silence was good for me rather than troubling. But she didn't know that. All she knew was that we weren't speaking, and she let it go on for nine full months.

If your narcissistic mother does contact you, then I can (almost) guarantee how it'll go. She'll most likely contact you cheerfully, with *zero* reference to all that went before, as if you had parted in great form only a day or two previously.

So how do you react?

If you want to keep in contact with her, it's probably best to play along with her cheerful tone. Answer her equally cheerfully and superficially. Make no reference to the previous quarrel. Pretend it never happened. Trying to discuss it so you can come up with a better understanding between you just will not work. She's a narcissist. It'd be like trying to reason with a toddler.

However, be prepared to fight the same battle the next time she wants you to do something you don't want to do. That'll be the crunch event. It could be that the fallout from the first incident exhausted you so much that you want to never go through it again, which is a perfectly valid response—I do stress that. But that will mean you're conceding a lifetime of never standing up to her ever. You'll have won the battle and lost the war.

There is good news, though. If you do stand up to your mother again, she'll learn that you mean what you say. This time the silent treatment will probably last a much shorter period of time, if it happens at all. And you're well on your way to reclaiming your autonomy. Go you!

Hugs,
Danu

FLYING MONKEYS SWOOP IN

Dear DONM,

During the silent treatment, your mother might send in the "flying monkeys."

This term comes from *The Wizard of Oz*, in which the witch sends out malevolent flying monkeys to do her bidding. The flying monkeys that your narcissistic mother sends out will most likely not be malevolent but misguided. They've only heard her side of the story, don't forget. Therefore, they're going to plead with you to give in to her.

This flying monkey will be someone who's close enough to your mother that they're in the blast zone for her frustration about your intransigence. By "your intransigence" I mean your fair boundaries calmly stated and enforced, of course. But your mother sees it as intransigence, and the flying monkey is repeating the official narrative.

As it's someone close, it might be your father or a sibling or an aunt—somebody like that. Very possibly someone you love, and whose respect you want, and whose well-being you desire. This person may well genuinely love you and want good things for you too. But if they're caught in your narcissistic mother's web (and they are, or they wouldn't be doing this), then what they want even more than that is for your mother to have her way. This could be because that'll give them a quiet life, or because they have genuinely been convinced of her side of the story. Or both, of course, along with possibly even other reasons. People are complex.

So they do not have your best interests at heart, no matter how much they present themselves that way. They have a mission to bring you back into the fold on your narcissistic mother's terms, no matter the personal cost to you. They'll do whatever it takes to do that.

They might use scolding: "How can you be so mean to your mother?" They might use guilt: "She's so upset, you know. She's crying all the time." They might use variations of those.

So how do you deal with it?

You can either say, "I'm not going to discuss my mother with you" (phrased more gently than that if needed, of course), or simply, "She's the one not talking to me, you know. I asked her to contact me when she was ready."

They might say, "Well, why don't you be the bigger person and contact her. She's too upset to contact you."

Don't fall for that! More about being the bigger person later, but for now, just don't fall for it!

Just repeat, "Well, she knows she is welcome to contact me whenever she wants."

If they insist, trying to get you to contact her, then they are stepping on your boundaries big-time and need to be stopped. You can say something like, "I appreciate your concern. But this is between me and her, so I'd prefer if we didn't discuss it any further."

Then do what you need to in order to enforce that. In a very real way, you'll be doing with the flying monkey what you did with your mother: stating fair boundaries and calmly enforcing them.

Sometimes the flying monkey will beg you to contact your narcissistic mother on the grounds that "she's taking it out on me, and I can't bear it anymore."

This is a tough one for sure. You don't want the flying monkey suffering. But here's the thing: it's not you making them suffer; it's your mother. The flying monkey is responsible for their own relationship with your mother; you are not responsible for that.

Listen to what they're really saying: "Can you please continue to suffer from her treatment so I don't have to?" Is that a fair thing to ask?

This might be the time to tell the flying monkey the truth about her so they understand. But maybe not—reread the letter about telling your siblings about narcissistic personality disorder before you make any decision.

The bottom line with flying monkeys, though, is that you are under no obligation to listen to them. Your mother sending them is just more manipulation (no matter whether she directly asked them to come or, more likely, manipulated the situation so they'd do it of their own accord). It's both unfair of them and on them to do this, and you are fully entitled not to facilitate this.

Be aware, though, that if you stand up to flying monkeys, they might well cut you off too, preferring to stand firmly in your mother's camp.

Sigh. All this because you didn't want to spend your birthday with her. But that's how these hideous dynamics go. More about this next.

Hugs,
Danu

LOSING THE FLYING MONKEYS TOO

Dear DONM,

Be aware that narcissistic mothers cleverly weave a very tight codependent web of their relationships. I visualize it as a literal web—with her the big, fat, malevolent spider in the middle, and everyone else stuck to the threads, trapped and arrayed around her. Some of those people will be struggling to get free (you, maybe), and others will be sitting quietly, acquiescent and accepting. Those others perhaps cannot even imagine their lives free, can't visualize a life lived without being in constant reference to her and her needs and moods and sulks and whims. They are comfortable with the status quo, as people tend to be, and are terrified of change.

If you make changes by standing up to your mother, you may well terrify them. Not only might they be suffering because she is taking her anger at you out on them, or inflicting her dramatic back-of-hand-to-forehead-and-take-to-the-chaise-longue-with-the-smelling-salts hurt on them, but you're also rocking their boat. You're upsetting the balance that has sustained them (no matter how poorly) all this time.

They might become annoyed with you too. It's far safer to be angry with you than to be angry with your mother. In a way, they are justified in being angry with you—you are the one making changes, after all.

There is a very real risk that if they are forced to choose between you and your mother, they'll choose your mother. Of course, you will not be the one forcing the choice; your mother will be. But she might well do that. She might say to them, "Well, if you're going to continue seeing her [meaning, you], then I want nothing to do with you." They would have to choose your mother, unless they're able to break free entirely.

So you do risk losing other people close to you by this process. It's unfair. It's completely and utterly unfair. All you wanted to do was spend your birthday your way, after all—something totally simple that most people take for granted, something absolutely reasonable. And now all this. But that's the way it goes when you have a narcissistic mother and codependent family.

Only you can decide if it's worth it.

The thing is, in a way it's not easy to make the decision now. You're probably still stuck to the web. You don't know how good life in freedom is. Take my word, and the experience of so many other DONMs—it is so worth it. Yes, there's a price to pay, and often it's a very high price. But freeDONM is wonderful and liberating and empowering and all sorts of good things.

Hugs,
Danu

BEING THE BIGGER PERSON

Dear DONM,

So, flying monkeys have the mission to bring you back into the fold on your narcissistic mother's terms, no matter the personal cost to you. They'll do whatever it takes.

One of their favorite tactics is often something along these lines:

"Yes, I know she's being unreasonable. But you know what she's like. So, come on, be the bigger person here. Tell her you're sorry, even though we both know you did nothing wrong. It'll make her happy and we can all get along again."

Be the bigger person. Right.

Be the bigger person, with the implication that if you hold your position, then you're a small person, a narrow, bigoted, petty person. That the mature thing to do is to pander to her. It won't take much, after all—just a pro-forma apology in the interests of keeping the family together. It's not so much to ask, is it?

Put like that, it's hard to refute, especially, as I've already said, when it comes from someone you love.

What do you do?

Always with the caveat that you should do what *you* decide and what *you* want and what *you* think is best, you need to know that you have no obligation to fall for this.

You might choose to concede. That's your right, of course.

But you have no obligation to.

In a way the flying monkey most likely will not appreciate, you are already being the bigger person. You are being the one who is big enough (i.e., adult enough) to calmly state and enforce a boundary. You are the one being mature enough to step outside dysfunction and manipulation, to stop playing toxic games. To say: "I do not wish to do x and I will not."

Even if that were not so, you have no obligation to be the bigger person. In healthy relationships people are equally big. "Be the bigger person" is just a euphemism for "let her continue to treat you exactly as she wishes while you roll over and take it," and you have no obligation whatsoever to do that.

The flying monkey is being disingenuous to dress that up as some kind of virtue—and even more disingenuous to dress it up as their concern for your mother when it is most likely about their own wish to no longer experience the fallout of your mother's drama and fury.

You are perfectly within your rights to say calmly to the flying monkey, "I don't need to be a bigger person if it means apologizing for something I didn't do. I appreciate you trying to sort it out, but this is between her and me, and it's best left that way."

It's totally your right to establish boundaries with the flying monkey just as much as with your narcissistic mother.

Hugs,
Danu

WHAT ABOUT YOUR OTHER RELATIONSHIPS?

Dear DONM,

As you grow and heal from your narcissistic upbringing, you might experience pushback from people around you. Not just from your narcissistic mother (if you're still in touch with her) or her flying monkeys, but from other people as well. Your significant other or partner, for example. Or your best friends. Or colleagues.

They may start complaining about you: "I don't know what's got into you. You're being awfully snarky lately." Or even "You're being very selfish lately."

There are two possibilities here.

The first is that, unfortunately, that relationship is toxic too. I'm sorry to say this, as I know it's not easy to hear. (And it might not be so anyway; see below.) But the fact is that DONMs can often find themselves in other abusive relationships as well. It's what we know, after all. It's what we're trained for. Abusers can find us to be good fodder and are attracted to us for that reason.

Of course, an abuser isn't going to want you to find your power and so will do all in their power to try to put you back in your box when you start becoming assertive.

The second possibility is that they are not abusers at all, but even so, they are threatened by the changes in you. It makes sense: they fell in love with you/got to know you as you were, and here you are changing. They liked the old way better.

They liked being able to have things their way all the time, and don't want that to change. That's understandable, and even decent non-abusive people can struggle with that.

Also, change is scary for people—even good change. And this is change they haven't chosen and are not steering, and they don't know where they'll end up. They might fear that you will leave them if this carries on, that you might outgrow them. No wonder they resist that change and maybe even try to sabotage it.

And you know, they might be right about you outgrowing them. Once you start to grow and stretch, you most likely won't want to shrink to fit ever again. You start to expect more and better. Sometimes even genuinely well-meaning people cannot provide that.

So there are lots of reasons why those close to you might resist your growth. You need to decide if you want to continue growing regardless of their resistance. Not in a nasty-selfish way, but in a birthright kind of way. It's a valid choice to stay small, to not rock the boat. I'm not advocating one or the other, as that wouldn't be my place; I just want to lay out the possibilities and potential issues for you.

So those who are near to you might resist your growth, either because they're abusers or because they're ordinary, scared people. Don't be surprised if that happens, and maybe think ahead of time about how you'll react if/when they do.

The harsh fact is that you might find that some relationships die during this process.

My own marriage ended after I cut off contact with my parents. The no contact gave me space to look at a marriage that, frankly, had never worked. We both (me more than him, I have to say, but him too) had been trying to salvage the unsalvageable since forever.

It was never an abusive relationship; that was good luck rather than good planning, as I was well primed for emotional abuse. My ex was, and is, a fundamentally decent man. However, our marriage was dysfunctional (as in, not working) from Day 1. Looking back, I see that it was codependent.

So my marriage ended as part of this journey, and other relationships have ended too. This has been very painful. The past years have been absolute hell for me in so many ways. I cannot promise that, once on this path, the same or something similar won't happen to you too.

But you know what? I wouldn't change a thing. The price has been horrendous, but the gifts have been beyond wonderful. I'm so much stronger now, so much better balanced. I'm learning and growing and increasing in happiness and peace. And I believe things will continue to get better, as the worst of the upheaval is over and I'm starting to reap more benefits of the growth. The changes are intoxicating in their possibilities, and so empowering.

Yes, a data point of one (i.e., me) is not statistically significant. But it is all I have to share, after all. I haven't conducted a whole study on this. You need to make your decisions for you, and I wish you courage and fortitude for those decisions. The problem is that you have to pay the price without knowing the rewards. The caterpillar cannot envision what it is like to be a butterfly, and how she will fly free and beautiful, even as her body liquefies to a pulp first.

I just know that I love flying, and I love my bright colorful wings.

Hugs,
Danu

MORE ABOUT GUILT

Dear DONM,

You may not be long on this journey before you consider cutting down contact as much as possible with your narcissistic mother (known as low contact), or even cutting off contact with her entirely (known as no contact).

There is a lot of information about these topics in *You're Not Crazy*, but what I want to talk about now is how you feel about all of this. If you are like most DONMs, you will feel a huge sense of guilt at even the prospect of cutting down contact or cutting off contact.

This is totally understandable. There are a lot of strands conspiring to make you feel like this. Apart from Stockholm syndrome (also known as trauma bonding), as discussed in *You're Not Crazy*, there are four other strands that I can see.

The first is your own mother's brainwashing, which makes you feel responsible for her. (We'll be talking a lot more about this.) The second is your love for her, if you have that. The third is your desire to please her and keep her happy and maybe win her love that way. The fourth is society's attitude toward mothers: society reveres mothers, it puts them on a pedestal, and woe to the woman who dares to say the emperor has no clothes or the mother is not perfect.

I have read an observation that society's need to believe in the mother myth is so strong that our fairy tales feature bad stepmothers, not bad mothers. These ancient stories wanted to explore the topic of bad mothers but could not do so directly. Nowadays anyone who dares to say she is not in touch with her mother gets a metaphorical (or maybe even literal) hissing intake of breath, as the disapproval is plainly shown. It's hard to go against that. I remember being on a radio interview when *You're Not Crazy* first came out, and I explained how my relationship with my mother was an abusive one, and that's why I left it. Even after all that, the presenter asked me at the end would I not try to sort things out with my mother.

I said, "If you had a woman on your show who had an abusive partner, and after years and years of trying to sort things out, and being beaten down at every turn, had finally managed to escape from him, would you ask her about trying to sort things out with him?"

The presenter, to his credit, got immediately what I was saying and conceded that he would not.

But society doesn't acknowledge that there can be abusive mother-daughter relationships, and so to admit that you are not in touch with your mother (or only in rare contact, in limited circumstances) is absolute heresy.

All this adds to the feelings of guilt, and that guilt can keep you trapped in this abusive relationship. This is an abusive relationship, make no mistake. If your mother is narcissistic, a healthy, loving, mutually supportive relationship is not possible. But you might know that logically but not feel it.

The guilt you feel is real. I do not invalidate it. It's very real. But it is not true. It is not justified. Guilt is for when we do something wrong, and protecting yourself from an abuser can never be wrong. Yes, that abuser might be dressed up as your mother, wearing a pretty mask, fooling society and even you. But she's still an abuser.

I suggest that when you feel the guilt, you observe it as if from a safe distance. It's a bit of a psychological trick that is very helpful and very doable. Observing an emotion helps distance you from it a bit, rather than swimming, and even drowning, in it. Notice that you are feeling this guilt. Take the time to find out where in your body this guilt is sitting. What size is it? Shape? Texture? (It will have a location in your body, and when you examine it, a size, shape, and texture.)

The guilt feels like your enemy, making you feel bad. But it is actually your friend, trying to help you, trying to make sure you don't do the wrong thing. It just has incorrect information about what the wrong thing is. So—and this may sound really silly; in fact I'm sure it does!—I recommend that you talk to the guilt. The guilt is a part of your brain, so it's really you talking to you, so it's not as crazy as it sounds. Say something like: "Guilt, I know you are trying to help me here by making me feel bad for cutting off contact with my mother. But there is no need for me to feel guilty, I promise you. You have false information. I am doing nothing wrong here. I ask you to let go of me now."

Over time the feelings of guilt should fade.

One way, of course, of speeding up this process, is to use EFT. Whichever way you do this, I invite you to free yourself from the untrue guilt. You deserve no less.

Hugs,
Danu

THE NEED TO BELONG

Dear DONM,

The need for humans to belong is very, very strong. Indeed, psychologist Abraham Maslow in his famous Hierarchy of Needs put the need to belong as one of our highest needs, just behind survival needs such as safety, food, and shelter.

This makes perfect sense, of course. For most of human history, belonging to a tribe was an essential survival strategy. This is because we are weak and defenseless alone, and it is only as part of a tribe that we can survive.

Even now a human would struggle to survive without the help and infrastructure provided by other humans. Technically, in this more formal world, we could survive with only the help and assistance of strangers. But it doesn't feel like that—we still feel the need for our tribe. In this way, the need to belong does not come *after* the other survival needs—it is *another* survival need. No wonder we feel it so strongly.

But DONMs then have a big problem. We often feel that we do not belong anywhere at all. It is understandable as we, in a very real sense, did not belong in our own families. We were not welcome there; we were not cherished and nurtured as a valuable and important family member. No wonder we struggle sometimes to belong in the world. Or rather, to feel as if we belong in the world, because we do belong in the world, just as much as anyone else.

I think this sense of not belonging can be a self-fulfilling prophecy in ways. We believe we don't belong, that we're not good enough—and somehow we project that belief, and others pick up on it and react to it. Now, this is only my own theory, I have to stress, based on my own experiences.

I used EFT to make myself feel that I belonged better in group situations, and it did change my experiences in groups. Whether people literally responded better to me or whether I just felt they did (and maybe they had never responded badly; maybe that was just my perception) didn't seem to matter. I felt that I belonged there, and that's what seemed to happen.

So I suggest you use EFT for this. Feeling like you belong makes a big difference to so many experiences, and it's well worth pursuing. In truth, it's no less than we deserve.

Hugs,
Danu

SELF-CARE STRUGGLES

Dear DONM,

One of the worst aspects of the DONM legacy is that often we don't look after ourselves properly. We either neglect our own self-care or we actively sabotage ourselves. The punishment can take forms like nail-biting or eating the wrong foods, or it can be as severe as self-cutting.

I used to struggle with basic self-care. I did it, don't get me wrong; the desire to be socially acceptable made sure of that. But I had to force myself to do it. It was like climbing a mountain every single time. It was exhausting. Taking all that energy to do really basic stuff meant I had that much less energy left for actually living.

I think it's understandable when you've been raised as we have, especially if you had an Ignoring mother who neglected your care needs. The message deeply ingrained is: "You're not worth looking after. You don't deserve to have your self-care needs met. You're not valuable enough to be cared for."

Then, when we reach adulthood, we take over her job for her. It's a perversion of the normal situation. In a healthy situation the mother cares for the child until the child is big enough, and then the mother hands over the job of caring for the child to the child herself, and the child takes on that job. It all happens very naturally and gradually, with ever-increasing amounts of responsibility handed to the child as she's ready for them.

The same thing happens to us but, as I say, in a perverted way. The narcissistic mother's "job" is to neglect and abuse us, and she hands that over to us, and we naturally and without realizing it accept the job. It's all we know, and all we think we're worth.

When I say "think," it's not that we rationalize this or do it on a conscious level. It's all on a very subconscious level. But the result is the same: we take over her job of neglecting ourselves or abusing ourselves. That training, that indoctrination, runs deep, and it's a place where I think EFT comes into its own. I try to offer other alternatives to EFT where possible, because I don't want to just always push EFT or make it seem like the only option. But in this case, I have not found anything that works as well to change such deeply entrenched behavior and thinking.

Whatever you decide, I do hope you'll find it easier to care for yourself, as you truly deserve that.

Hugs,
Danu

WHAT ABOUT YOUR HAPPINESS?

Dear DONM,

Happiness is something that's often been on my mind. I think it's probably something that's on everybody's mind. Happiness is what we humans seek, after all. All of us—not just DONMs. We seek it in objects and experiences and relationships.

The trick, I know, is to feel happy regardless of external circumstances. Far easier said than done. It's a journey I'm still on, one during which I stumble often.

The Buddhists are right, I think, in that it's attachment that causes suffering. There is only one thing that makes me unhappy: that I want something and cannot have it. Whether that's my mother's love, or a healthy family dynamic, or something trivial like a new dress, it is the mismatch between wanting it and not having it that makes me unhappy.

One solution is to get every single thing we want. But of course, that's not realistic. Many things, such as wanting love from a narcissistic mother, are out of our hands to obtain. Others, such as material goods, are limited due to finances, but in truth they don't make us really happy even if we get them, as we always want the next thing.

The other option, the Buddhist one, is to release all desires. If you didn't want anything, ever, you wouldn't be unhappy. I'm not sure that works either. Even if we could release all desires, is that really ideal? It is part of the richness of our human experience to want, to desire, to aspire, to seek. We'd all be still living in caves otherwise.

The trick, I believe, is to separate our happiness from our desires. Have desires, by all means, and strive to reach them. But do not make happiness conditional upon reaching them.

I think what I'm trying to say is that it's a good goal to keep happiness and desires on parallel paths, rather than intertwined, for them to be independent of each other.

As it is, we put conditions on happiness. "I'll be happy when I get x" is the thinking. But the corollary of that is that we can't be happy unless we have x.

And it's never-ending. Say we get x. It will make us happy, that's true. But only for a while. A very interesting study found that really good events like winning the lottery, and really bad events like becoming paralyzed, did indeed respectively raise, and lower, one's happiness levels, just as you'd expect. But, interestingly, happiness levels only changed temporarily. After a year, the happiness levels of the individuals concerned were back to where they had been before that life-changing event. If the impact of such huge events last only a year, how much less would the impact of smaller events last? We get used to having x, and now are unhappy because we don't have y. It's never-ending.

The way to end it is, as I'm suggesting, to unhook happiness from these desires. To stop putting conditions on happiness. This takes discipline and intention, but is, I am convinced, a path worth taking. In a very real way, we simply make the decision to be happy in our lives as they are. Easier said than done, of course, but it truly is only a decision away. This is a bit do-as-I-say-not-as-I-do, as I struggle with this one. I know it is possible, though, as I have done it at times and it feels so good. I do have to keep remaking the decision, falling off the happiness wagon and then climbing back on. Perhaps one day I'll be able to make the final decision, but for now I know it is a good thing to aspire to and to try to do.

The topic of looking for happiness applies to everybody, but DONMs have specific challenges, so we'll be discussing those next.

Hugs,
Danu

MORE ABOUT HAPPINESS

Dear DONM,

We spoke about separating our desires from our happiness—making our happiness unconditional, in other words.

But there is one other issue that, it seems to me, comes up for DONMs.

Often it can seem dangerous to be happy. Not right. Stressful, as though some doom is going to fall because we're happy.

This can apply to DONMs whose mothers didn't like them being happy and took steps to make sure they weren't happy.

These mothers were (are) threatened by their daughters' happiness. A happy daughter is not 100 percent focused on her mother, for a start, as she's living her life and enjoying her happiness. And if she's not 100 percent focused on her mother, that's a lack of narcissistic supply for the mother. A happy daughter is also not as fearful or as cooperative.

These mothers would have taken steps to ensure that their daughters didn't experience happiness—or at least, not for long.

They might say things like, "Wipe that smile off your face or I'll wipe it off for you."

They might have launched into a tirade, a rage, a fight in order to spoil the happy mood.

Or they might, and this is the nastiest of them all, take away the source of their daughter's happiness.

The beloved puppy was given away. The ride to dance lessons disappeared so the dancing had to stop. The new friend was bad-mouthed enough that the friendship withered.

The tactics vary, of course, but the end result is the same—a daughter who subconsciously, and totally reasonably, believes that it is not safe to be happy.

The effect of this belief is that we cannot allow ourselves to be happy, which makes perfect sense, right? If it's not safe to be happy, we'd be crazy to let ourselves do the dangerous thing.

We very possibly feel stressed whenever we start to be happy, but this feeling is so normal and common that we don't even identify it as such. The result is that we damp down the happy feelings.

We might even subconsciously sabotage the things that make us happy, just as our mother did. There's a kind of irony in that, isn't there? We might be perfectly capable of getting ourselves to dance lessons now that we're an adult, but somehow we just stop going.

This is so, so sad, when we carry on our mother's role of abusing us. Our motivation is completely different, of course. But the result is the same.

As ever, EFT is the way to root out those stale incorrect beliefs, and I offer it to you as something to try if you find yourself feeling stressed or panicked at the thought or feeling of happiness. It will leave you able to feel good about feeling happy.

You can use EFT, tapping for the statement, "It's not safe to feel happiness," and see where that brings you, and then tap using statements that come up for you as you do that. Feeling safe about feeling happy is no more than your birthright, no matter that it was stolen from you. You deserve to reclaim it.

Hugs,
Danu

MORE ABOUT BELIEFS

Dear DONM,

In *You're Not Crazy* I spoke extensively of how our beliefs impact us in huge ways. I wish to expand on this now.

The fact is that our beliefs are integral to the quality of our lives. Our beliefs steer us. They're our programming, almost literally. Maybe *really* literally.

The trouble is that these beliefs are buried so deep down, and are so subtle, that we're not aware of their impact. Therefore, we cannot make conscious decisions as to whether to believe our beliefs or not, so to speak.

If our beliefs would speak to us clearly, it would be a lot easier. Say, for example, somebody invites you to make a presentation to leaders in your industry. If you could have a rational debate with your beliefs, they might say to you:

"Yeah, that sounds like a good opportunity, for sure. It'd be great to get to speak to them, and it would really raise your profile. But the thing is that it isn't safe for you to speak in public. They might laugh at you—they probably *will* laugh at you—if you make even the smallest mistake. Remember how your narcissistic mother always laughed at you when you did that, and how small it always made you feel? You don't want to experience that again, do you?"

You could then calmly consider all that.

And you might respond: "That's true. Good point. But I'll be able to prepare this speech, so the chances of making any mistakes are minimal. And if I do—well, these people aren't my narcissistic mother. They won't be so petty as to laugh. They'll know I'm not a professional speaker, so they won't be judging me on that, but on the quality of my content.

"And you know," you might continue as you consider it further, "if they did laugh, then that's okay. It would say far more about them than it does about me. I'm not that helpless child now; I am strong enough to survive, or even dismiss, their laughter."

You and your beliefs could have a reasoned, calm, adult discussion, and you could make a balanced decision about whether to give the presentation or not.

Your decision might even be: "You're right. I don't want to risk that. I'll turn down the opportunity." And that'd be okay. Either way, it'd be your conscious, considered, decision.

But that's not what happens. What really happens is this:

The offer is made. Your brain hears it and immediately sends it to the Beliefs Vault for evaluation. The belief that it'd be unsafe for you to speak in public comes rushing forward, warning frantically of the danger, and in order to protect yourself from that danger, your brain floods your system with feelings of stress and fear.

All this happens in an instant so that all you're aware of is the offer to speak, followed by instant, unidentified stress and fear. Next thing, you hear yourself turning down the offer as a knee-jerk reaction, or you agree to do it despite the knots in your stomach and spend the intervening time feeling ill at the prospect.

When it comes time to do the talk, it might go well, and a new belief will be forged about how you can do these things well.

More likely, the original belief might remain as you subconsciously think, "We got away with it that time because you didn't make any mistakes. But the danger still lurks. It could all go wrong the next time."

Or worse again, humans being what they are, you might even subconsciously sabotage the presentation in some way to prove to yourself that you were right about it being dangerous.

Do you see how it works? Your conscious, thinking, rational self doesn't get to make the decision at all (either to do it or not to do it). Your beliefs make the decision for you. They steer you. They steer you away from danger as they perceive it. They're your friend, trying to help you. The problem is that their assumptions about what's dangerous go unexamined.

It's very difficult to work against this system as it's so quick and so subtle. But there is good news. "By their fruits you shall know them," as the saying goes. Every time you want to do something and you don't, a belief is in play. Also, the more you get used to noticing the feelings and emotions, the more you'll know a belief is in play behind them.

EFT is terrific at exposing those beliefs. All you do is tap, in our example, on the statement "I want to do the presentation, and I don't." And as you tap, the beliefs will come up. The awareness will come to you: "They might laugh at me."

And then you tap on that statement: "They might laugh at me."

See what happens then. Either that belief will fade and ease, or the belief behind it (e.g., "I couldn't bear it if they laughed at me") will come up for examination and erasing using EFT.

In this way you get to examine all the beliefs that are running your life and eliminate those that aren't true and don't serve you.

Sometimes the resistance proves to have a really good reason, or belief, behind it. You might realize that your belief is that you're not ready for such a big presentation, and when you consider it calmly, you realize that, no, you're really not.

And that's okay. This way you're turning down the opportunity for well-considered and good reasons. In a very real way, you were able to have that discussion with your beliefs and able to make good decisions for good reasons. Nothing about this process is to make you automatically override your beliefs or reactions, but rather to examine them and make a conscious decision, taking into account all the facts.

You can also use this process to examine your beliefs as they relate to your narcissistic mother. There might be a belief like "I have to keep her happy" or "I cannot cope if she's angry with me." Are they true? Worth finding out!

Hugs,
Danu

SO, WERE YOU REALLY BORN BROKEN?

Dear DONM,

One of the most toxic gifts our narcissistic mother gives us, in my opinion, is the belief (which feels like way more than a belief—it feels like an unquestioned knowing, an absolute truth) that we were born broken: that from the moment of our birth there was something inherently flawed about us, something wrong, misshapen, grotesque. This is an extremely nasty form of cruelty, to take this perfect little baby and to dump on her all this psychic toxic sludge, so that when she looks in her mental mirror, it is the sludge she sees and not her own innate beauty.

And oh, all our flaws we're told about. I wouldn't mind, but in most cases they're not even our real flaws. My own parents didn't even know me well enough to know my real flaws. What they projected onto me was what they needed to project to keep me docile, to keep me "bad" so she could be "good." The flaws of oversensitivity and bad perceptions, among them.

Worse, there was always the specter of other flaws, which they knew and would reveal to me if they needed to. I called it the Horrible Danu Mirror. The threat was always there to show me what I really looked like, the toxic sludge being the least of it. And I couldn't bear to see how horrible they found me. My psyche was struggling enough with how horrible I already knew I was; I knew it couldn't cope with learning I was even worse than that. So I always caved at that threat, climbed back into my box, and let them continue to treat me as they wanted. It was a very powerful weapon in their hands.

Of course, the fact that I caved meant I never called their bluff, never realized they had nothing particularly bad about me, and I was not this gargoyle they tried to convince me I was. (The one time, toward the end of our relationship, when it went far enough that they did share how awful I was, guess what was the horrible thing about me? The fact that when they left my home after visits, I closed the door immediately instead of waving until they were out of sight as I should. Seriously.)

No wonder I—and other DONMs too, I know—grew up with the absolute belief that we were born broken, that we were intrinsically damaged. That's a tough burden to carry constantly. In a way it's like air pressure. Humans don't consciously experience air pressure because we are used to it all our lives. But it's there, pressing down on us always. This belief in our born-broken-ness is always there, no matter that we are not consciously aware of it. It impacts everything, I think. I suspect I am not aware of *how much* it impacts, even now. But to carry this image of our own grotesqueness into the world has to impact how we present ourselves to others, how much we are willing to risk, the value we place on ourselves.

The good news is that this belief is just that—a belief. And it's a false belief. We're no more broken than anyone else. We're not perfect, for sure, but averagely flawed like other people. Not grotesque and horrific and monstrous. So, it's a false belief and, therefore, one that can be changed by using EFT, or even without EFT. If you prefer not to use EFT, I invite you to use affirmations: "I am well. I am whole. I am fine just as I am." Repeat these as often as you can to reprogram your brain. (The EFT does work a lot more quickly and deeply, though.)

Hugs,
Danu

A SMALL OBSERVATION ON THOUGHTS

Dear DONM,

A recurring theme of these letters is this:

1) Our beliefs are programmed into our brains by our experiences and what we were taught.
2) Therefore, they create our feelings and thoughts, which control what actions we take.
3) The actions we take control our results and the quality of our lives.

I am forever going on about how we can use EFT to change our beliefs and so have that cascade of effects work in our favor rather than against us.

But using EFT takes time, and it can be hard to remember to use it. So here is a handy trick for other occasions:

You cannot help or control what thoughts come to you. They are born of your programmed beliefs. But you absolutely can control the thoughts you have about those thoughts. You can have layers of thoughts, in other words. You can step a little bit aside from the programmed thought and observe it, judge it, and consider it. Then you can decide what you will do next, whether you will believe the programmed thought or not, whether you'll act according to it or not.

So, if your automatic thought is something like "They'll all laugh at me if I do that," then you can consider that objectively: *Will* they laugh at you? Will they really?

Then the answer will come from reality and not your programmed beliefs.

The answer might be "No, they won't," in which case you can go ahead and do whatever that belief was blocking.

Or it could be "Yes, they will," because not all programmed beliefs are wrong, of course. But then you can examine that thought too. Maybe ask yourself, "Does it matter if they do? Maybe I could carry on regardless. Maybe I don't care about their opinion—or not enough to stop me anyway."

Or you might decide that, yes, it does matter that they will laugh at you, and therefore you won't do it. But that's okay. The purpose of this exercise is not to make you do things you don't want to. It's to let you examine thoughts and beliefs, judge them, and make a clear, conscious decision about them. It's about you choosing your actions from a place of clarity and consideration, rather than as a knee-jerk response. In that is your power.

Hugs,
Danu

IS IT REALLY YOUR JOB
TO FIX EVERYTHING?

Dear DONM,

Another lie by narcissistic mothers is that it's our job to fix things. This manifests as parentification when we are children—expecting us to take the parent's role so she can take the child's role. Many of us grow up to be regular fixers, feeling responsible for everything.

As soon as we hear of our mother having any problems, we don our superhero cloak and off we go.

So, we have a situation where, for example, if two of our siblings aren't talking to each other, we feel obliged to fly from one to the other, like the diplomatic corps, sorting it all out. Or if our mother has run out of her medication—totally through her own fault—it's we who have to drive all over town to try to get a new supply for her.

This sense of responsibility, that it's our job to make sure everything works okay, is a real trap. And of course, it's not true. We are responsible for certain things, for sure, but most of them are about our own life: our own children, our own house, our job. We're not responsible for others' lives.

But yet, when we feel we are, that's the trap, isn't it?

We don't think we have the choice of whether to help solve the problem or not—we feel obliged to. And that's exhausting.

The other problem with that is, with the games narcissists play, if we help out with a project, then we suddenly become responsible for the success of that project forever. So if our mother needed our help in finding a new house to buy, and ended up buying one that we found for her—well, any problems with the house, going forward forever, would be our fault. Conveniently forgotten would be the fact that we just gave her the information about it, and that she was the one who chose to buy it. No, the leaky plumbing and loud neighbors would be our fault.

Or maybe we did encourage her to buy it. Maybe that was part of what we had to fix. Maybe she was playing helpless, not able to make a decision, so we did suggest she buy it, in all good faith of course. And so, then it's definitely our fault.

It's a win for the narcissistic mother, of course—she has you running around at the time of the purchase and gains a stick to beat you with going forward.

The only way out of this trap is to stop feeling responsible for fixing everything. To decline the responsibility.

One way to do this is to stop responding to veiled hints that there's a job for you to fix. So if your mother says, "Alex and Sheila aren't speaking," instead of responding that you'll speak to them both and sort it out, you say mildly and, above all, in a noncommittal tone, "Oh dear, I'm sorry to hear that."

If she then becomes more direct and says, "Would you have a word with them? You're so good at getting them to see sense," you can answer something like, "Ah, they're adults, they can sort out their own issues."

If she insists, maybe laying on the guilt, "But it upsets me so much to see them fighting" (trying to get you to be a flying monkey), you can respond with sympathy, "Yes, I'm sure it does. That's hard for you, I have no doubt."

It might seem hard to just let her stay upset rather than trying to solve the matter, but another, overlapping lie is that we're responsible for her happiness.

We'll be discussing this more in the next letter. For now, just know that if she's unhappy about anything, well, she's responsible for her feelings, not you. You can empathize about her upset, but you don't have to take it away.

If the thing you're expected to fix is something urgent, like her medication, you might make the choice of getting it for her this time, as it's a safety issue, but stressing to her that you will not do this again. That she needs to plan ahead to make sure she doesn't run out, and if she doesn't do that, she will be responsible for that. Or that she needs to put a system in place that ensures she gets it automatically, to avoid both the drama games and your drop-everything-else involvement.

I know that's difficult, but if she is playing these games, then she's the one taking chances with her health, not you. (Of course, you always have the choice to play her game in this example. None of this is about taking away your choices, but to hopefully make you see that you do have different options for how to respond.)

If she asks you straight out to fix something, you might like to cultivate the habit of saying, "I'll think about that and get back to you." That gives you space to consider it properly in your own time, without the spell that these narcissistic mothers can cast. None of this is to say that you can't help or that you shouldn't help. It's so you can avoid feeling automatically obliged to help, or feeling guilty if you don't.

She won't like you applying that boundary, of course. She might try to insist that you answer her now. One way to solve this is to say, "If you insist on an answer now, the answer will be no."

If she does insist, then do tell her no, and keep to that decision. That way, you teach her that you mean what you say, and therein lies your power when she realizes she cannot bully you as she used to.

Then, in your own space and time, think calmly about the request and decide if it's appropriate for you to do.

As ever, this feeling about it being your job to fix things is deeply ingrained, and as ever, I offer you the tool of EFT to erase it.

Hugs,
Danu

IS IT REALLY YOUR JOB
TO MAKE HER HAPPY?

Dear DONM,

We spoke of how it's our job (so we're taught) to fix everything. The carrot for doing that well is our mother's approval (always temporary and conditional); the stick is her unhappiness. That feeds right into another belief we were fed: the belief that we are responsible for her happiness, or lack thereof.

Like the other lies she taught us, we believed it totally and in many cases are still living by it. This is why it's so easy for her to make us feel guilty for lots of things—because if the right thing is to make her happy, then obviously, if we are not making her happy, we're wrong—and the guilt is for doing wrong. (The thing is, as I often say, this guilt is real, for sure, but it is not true. It is not justified.)

We are talking about the belief that we have to do whatever it takes, no matter the price to us, to keep her happy.

We are talking about the belief that if she has a problem, no matter the source of it, it is our responsibility to solve it. Even if she is the source of the problem through her actions, we must (according to this narrative) protect her from the consequences of her own actions and solve the problem. Or if the problem is not solvable, we must at least pander to her upset about the problem, operate the workarounds the problem demands, and so on. An example of this might be that if she has ill health because she won't follow doctors' advice, we have to run around getting her special foods or painkillers at a moment's notice and/or spend hours listening to her complaining about her illness.

We're talking about the fact that her tiniest wants take precedence over our own wants, or even our needs.

An example of that might be that she wants to be present in the delivery room when we give birth, and we allow it even though we really don't want her there at the time, because if we say no, she will be unhappy, and we are responsible for her happiness.

This belief can even lead us to put her happiness above our own children's needs: for example, their birthday parties being spoiled because she wanted to be at them, and of course then made them all about her.

The thing is that like so much else, this belief is a lie. One of her many lies. The fact is that we are not responsible for our mother's well-being and happiness. We are not responsible for the well-being and happiness of any other adult except perhaps a spouse (and even then, that responsibility is limited). Yes, we are responsible for our own behavior, and it is not right to proactively do wrong things to others. But that is not what we're talking about here.

We are not responsible to make her happy or keep her happy. If we make decisions that are in our best interests, it does not matter that they make her unhappy—again, with the only proviso that we do not do anything proactively unethical to her. So, of course, I'm not talking about it making you happy to hit her! I'm talking about decisions you make about your own life.

This motto is so true: "If one of us has to be unhappy, it doesn't have to be me." You, no doubt, are unhappy with many of the hoops you have to jump through to keep her happy. The solution lies in letting go of the belief that it's your responsibility to make and keep her happy. There is huge freedom in that. You can start making decisions in your own best interests, and if she is unhappy, so be it.

It is not that you will take pleasure in her unhappiness, but rather that you will be able to witness it calmly, knowing that it is her responsibility to make and keep herself happy, and if she is failing in that responsibility to herself, it is not your problem.

Let me repeat that: It is not your problem.

Now, she'll try to make it your problem. Have no doubt about that. She'll rage, or weep, or cajole, or try to manipulate, or send flying monkeys—or a combination of these.

But it's still not your problem, and the more you can know that deep down, the freer you will be. You can calmly observe the rage, the tears, the sulks, and so on, without falling for them. Therein lies your freedom and your power.

So, how to get to that place where you no longer believe it's your job to keep her happy?

As we have been discussing, you can examine that belief when it pops up. Or you can keep telling yourself that it's not your job to keep her happy—repeat it like an affirmation. Or fake it till you make it: ask yourself, "What would I do in this moment if it were not my job to keep her happy?" Then do that, and ignore the churning stomach and thudding heart.

Or, as ever, I offer you EFT. That will help you delete and erase that programmed belief so you don't have to fake it—it will be real.

However you do it, it is so worthwhile to free yourself from the belief that you're responsible for her happiness. That, then, frees you to be responsible for your own happiness, which is as it should be.

Hugs,
Danu

ALL ABOUT POWER

Dear DONM,

Power. It's a loaded word, isn't it?

You may have even had a gut reaction when you read it.

I think that as DONMs, we're often scared of our own power. Our experience of power is that it's something to be abused, something used to injure people rather than help and support them.

No wonder we're scared of it. It seems like a monstrous thing, an out-of-control thing, a very dangerous thing. No wonder we can be prone to avoiding it. To prefer to remain safely, as we see it, in our powerlessness.

Now, when I say "as we see it," I mean, of course, as our subconscious sees it. This isn't a rational or considered decision, but it's no less real and no less binding on us for that.

I think there are two possible fears (again, they're not articulated, so they are formless and imprecise). The first is this: maybe we fear that we might become a nasty abusive person ourselves, if we had access to that power. This makes sense because we have only seen power abused, and never experienced power used for good. So it feels at a deep level that the only thing that keeps us decent and kind is that we have no other options, that inside us is an abusive monster, needing only the right weapon, in the form of power, to burst forth from us like the creature in the movie *Alien*. And of course, we like being decent and kind and all those good things. Of course, we don't want to be like our narcissistic abuser.

And so, we avoid that risk at all costs—and it is at all costs, pretty much, as remaining powerless leaves us weak and vulnerable by definition. It leaves us ineffective in the world. Which, again, is a situation we don't want—but it's better (so goes the subconscious argument) than the alternative.

The other fear, which I suspect runs parallel with the first one (so it's not an either/or; it's both), is that, even if there is no monster/abuser lurking, that power is inherently too dangerous. That it's too big for us to handle. That it'll run amok all by itself, regardless of our good intentions.

When I think of this concept, I always imagine myself being suddenly put in charge of, say, an F14 jet plane. Think of all that power—certainly too much power for my levels of competence and skill. Think of the death and destruction I would unwittingly cause by trying to harness that much power. It is terrifying to consider, isn't it? I shudder at the thought. Much, much better, and safer for everyone, and more sensible, for me to avoid being in charge of an F14.

We can apply the same logic to the concept of power. We can consider that we would be too incompetent at being in control of power itself, and that it is much better, and safer, and more sensible, to avoid all power.

See if you can use EFT to work on this topic if it's an issue for you. When you visualize yourself being powerful, what image comes up? I used to visualize myself as a giant walking past houses only as tall as my knee, and as I walked through the town, I wreaked destruction without meaning to, knocking over the houses through the clumsiness of my sheer size. I tapped on that image and slowly it faded, until now when I think of myself as being powerful, I just feel ordinary sized but strong, and I don't see myself causing any damage. In this way I can safely access my power. You might also find this exercise useful.

Or as ever, the option remains to look at this topic without EFT and simply affirm, journal, and so on about your relationship with power. It's worth resolving one way or another. We are no use to anyone—not ourselves, nor anyone else—if we are powerless.

Hugs,
Danu

VICTORY OVER YOUR NARCISSISTIC MOTHER

Dear DONM,

One of the most horrendous aspects to the narcissistic abuse is that our narcissistic mothers teach us to abuse ourselves. In a very real way we take over her job for her. We don't do this consciously, of course, nor deliberately. But the result is the same: we abuse ourselves just as she abused us.

We do this in various ways—for example, by speaking as abusively to ourselves as she did. Perhaps out loud; more likely and more insidiously and hence dangerously, quietly, in the privacy of our own heads in abusive self-talk.

Every time you think, "You're so stupid," or "You'll never be good enough," or "They won't like you," or "You're crazy to think you'll succeed at that," or "You're so fat," or "You're so clumsy," or "You never do anything right," you're doing her abuse for her.

It also manifests in our behaviors. Every time you over-eat, or undereat, or drink too much, or smoke, or don't bother to clean yourself or your home, you are continuing the abuse.

Every time you don't celebrate your successes, you are continuing her abuse.

Every time you don't give yourself time or space to mourn your losses and honor those appropriately, you are continuing her abuse for her.

It's like the abuse is a baton, and she passed it to you, and you took it and carried it forth.

Victory, therefore, lies in changing that pattern.

It's not easy, I know. Because when I say "you," I mean me too. I'm not immune from this. They say we teach what we need to learn, and I'm on this journey too. I'm writing what I need to hear as well.

And so, for us all, victory lies in changing the pattern. In treating ourselves well. In speaking to ourselves kindly. In feeding ourselves well. In meeting our needs and even our appropriate wants.

This is not just good because it's right for us. It's good because it's victory over that nasty woman. The only victory we'll get. We won't get an apology from her. We won't get recompense. We won't get acknowledgment from her, or from anyone else, most likely.

But victory is possible. Beating her is possible. Winning this battle is possible.

And so, if it feels hard to do the right thing for yourself for your own sake, maybe do it as a gesture of defiance to her.

Every time we make the higher decision, the self-care decision, we can think with satisfaction: "You didn't win, you [fill in expletive of choice here]. You didn't defeat me. I am winning with every good decision I make."

And there can be satisfaction in that.

Hugs,
Danu

THE CURSE OF POLITENESS

Dear DONM,

I've written before about how normal rules don't apply with narcissists—in other words, we don't have to obey etiquette rules such as sending a thank-you note for a gift. I'd like to explore this further, as the concept has been rearing its head for me recently.

A few days ago, I was reading comments on a blog post. A commenter said that he and his wife teach self-defense for women, and what they find is that the easy part is teaching the defensive moves; the difficult part is getting women to use their voices loudly.

And then I was speaking only last night to someone who teaches self-defense, and he has the same problem: that one of the biggest things he has to teach is a politeness bypass. I love that phrase: *politeness bypass.*

It reminds me of how, many years ago, I worked for a group setting up a Stay Safe program for schoolchildren, which aimed to teach them to protect themselves against possible pedophiles. One of the steps was to yell "NO!" Not to just say it, not even to say it firmly, but to yell it.

These things all have in common that they are counter to the normal rules of society, which include that we must be polite and agreeable. Women, especially, are taught from birth to be polite and agreeable. DONMs are taught even more: not just to be polite and agreeable, but to be cooperative and docile. There are good reasons to be polite and agreeable. We humans are a cooperative species. That's how we came to survive—all of our intelligence and opposable thumbs would be of little or no use to any one of us on our own. But unconditional politeness is a trap, in my opinion.

Politeness is a contract. It acknowledges that we're both (i.e., me and the person I'm engaging in the politeness with) members of a cooperative species, and here we are manifesting that cooperation. When it works, it works well. But it needs both parties to be polite for it to work as intended.

What we need to learn, and to learn well and powerfully, is that it's equally important to not be polite when that is appropriate. If the other person breaks the politeness contract, we are under no obligation to keep to it further. I think we need to learn this as women as well as DONMs. We need to learn it as mothers too, as we do our children no favors if we teach them that politeness is an absolute. Inappropriate politeness leaves us weak and vulnerable. Appropriate rudeness gives us strength.

By "rudeness" I don't mean proactive rudeness. I don't think there's ever a place for proactive rudeness. But it's definitely okay to answer rudeness with lack-of-politeness, and if society construes that as rudeness, so be it.

So, for example, if somebody gropes you on a crowded train, it would be appropriate to state loudly, "You need to take your hand off me, NOW." Yes, society doesn't like that, or permit it, really. But that rule by society allows people to grope us with impunity.

If someone knocks on your door looking for you to listen to their pitch, they are hijacking your time. They are being rude first. You don't have to be polite by standing there listening to them when you're not interested in what they're selling. You don't have to be nasty, but in my opinion it's okay to be firm: "I have no interest in this topic, so I'm going to go now. Goodbye." And then close the door.

The bad guys depend on our politeness. They use it against us. And that's whether it's a mild situation, such as salesmen at the front door, or an extremely bad one, such as a predator.

Our defense is to give ourselves permission to stop being polite when that's needed.

We'll talk more about this, including coming up with a strategy for how to implement it.

Hugs,
Danu

IT MIGHT NOT WIN YOU
AN OSCAR, BUT . . .

Dear DONM,

We've spoken about how sometimes you need a politeness bypass. Now, this is often easier said than done. As we said, as women we're trained by society to be polite and cooperative, and as DONMs, doubly so. Being appropriately impolite (assertive) can be difficult to do and can feel very strange, or even threatening.

The first thing to know is that when we're stressed, our mind struggles to think calmly and strategically. When that happens, it reverts to what it knows. And what it knows is politeness and acquiescence. Those are the default positions, so at a time of stress we automatically are polite and acquiescent, which is often the exact opposite of what's needed under the circumstances. The time to practice the new skills is when we are not under stress.

So I suggest that you rehearse these assertive moves. Rehearsing teaches your body to do it so it'll be easy to use when needed. Rehearsal is an amazing tool. There's a reason athletes and actors rehearse so diligently. It literally teaches your body what to do.

So, practice the skills. Practice being assertive with door-to-door salespeople by opening a door, for example, and saying, "No, thank you, I'm not interested. Goodbye," and closing it again. (Use an internal door rather than the front door if you don't want the neighbors thinking you've lost it entirely!)

Practice how you'll react to your narcissistic mother, depending on what you've decided is your preferred action. Say you've gone no contact and want to practice ignoring her if she's trying to get you to talk to her. Well, then, if possible, get somebody to act as her, imploring you to speak to her, or demanding, or whatever (try a few variations), as you simply ignore her. Or if you think your best bet would be to say, "I don't have anything to say to you. Go away," then practice that.

If you're still in touch with her, practice setting the boundaries you want to set. Again, if you can get someone to role-play her part, that'd be really good. If you can't get a co-actor, just imagine her.

This will all no doubt feel very silly: telling the air that you won't speak to it, for example. But it's a real process for a real reason. Actors often rehearse without props or co-actors too, just imagining them instead.

Practice using your voice, saying, "No, I won't do that" and similar boundary-setting phrases. Practice saying them loudly and sternly. You don't have to say them loudly and sternly in real life (although you might, if the occasion demands), but if you're able to say them loudly and sternly, then it's simple to ease back on that and say it more quietly when the time comes. This is just to get your body used to saying these things.

It's no use knowing in theory that you can be assertive and impolite. You have to own that behavior and have it available to you, and rehearsal is absolutely the way to do it.

Hugs,
Danu

THE GRIND

Dear DONM,

People often write to me to ask if healing from this upbringing is possible. I do believe that major recovery is possible, or I wouldn't be creating and sharing tools to help with that recovery. We are so lucky to live in a time when resources like EFT exist. Nowadays, recovery is far easier than at any previous time. We are also lucky to live in the age of the internet, which means we can learn about resources such as EFT and therapy, and also learn about narcissistic personality disorder to even know what was done to us.

However, it's also true that there is a lot of damage that has been done, damage that sometimes is hard even to quantify. What saddens me is the limitations that we're not even aware of, that confine us and squash us and make us tiny. The way we tell ourselves we cannot succeed, and think it's for real reasons but it's actually because we were never taught that success was allowed. Or maybe we were even expressly taught that success was *not* allowed for us. The way we think we're not deserving of love and think that's for real reasons, real flaws in us—not realizing that was part of the lies too.

That's one of the many things I love about EFT, that it brings those hidden beliefs to light. All you have to do is to tap for the circumstance you don't like (e.g., not being able to find a partner). When tapping, up will come the belief around that, and you can tap for that, and so on, until the truth is revealed, and it's always a healthier and more powerful truth than you first realized.

I've spoken of this before. But what I want to say today is how much I resent having to put so much time into fixing what my narcissistic mother and narcissism-enabling father broke. Into healing what they injured. Into trying to get myself sorted out enough to do what others take for granted. I'm tired of doing EFT! Yes, it's great, and I'm delighted to have it, but I'm so resentful of the necessity. It's so unfair that we DONMs have to work so hard to get from a minus to even a zero, to work so hard on healing all the stuff before we can start to achieve.

What really annoys me about this whole DONM thing is the sheer waste of it all. All those days and months and years we could have been doing worthwhile and fun stuff, and instead we spent all that time in a combination of pandering to her and in dealing with the fallout of our upbringing.

And even now, still dealing with the fallout, and for many of us, still pandering to her. The adventures we could have had, the career successes, the successful relationships, the rich friendships . . . and we either don't have them or, to get them, we have to work so incredibly hard.

I've seen ads along the way for athletic excellence, and the ones I recall have a theme of the athlete grinding away, putting the hours in when it's dark and cold and there's no glory or company or comfort. Doing what it takes so that when they get onto the field, they're fit and in peak condition. I think of DONMs when I see those, as we have to do the metaphorical equivalent of this training—not even to excel as the athletes do, but merely to cope, to be average in the world. So, yes, I think we can recover, but I'm not sure we'll ever recover fully. Who knows what our full height would have been. And even that recovery comes at a high price of effort and determination and grind. It's not fair.

Sorry to end on such a downbeat note. But it's not fair, and I do feel that, and sometimes it's good to acknowledge that too.

Hugs,
Danu

A SUGGESTION FOR YOU

Dear DONM,

I spoke just now of the grind—the work to heal ourselves, and how it's such a waste of time in some ways, and so unfair that it's necessary.

But given the reality that it *is* necessary if we want to heal, I want to share with you a very powerful exercise. It's very simple for something so powerful. Here's what you do:

Stand in front of a mirror, look at yourself straight in the eyes, and tap the EFT points in turn. That's it.

This exercise is both surprisingly difficult to do and also amazingly powerful. You will most likely struggle to meet your own eyes. It'll feel uncomfortable and wrong. It can feel very emotional, even overwhelmingly so. The tapping will add to the intensity of the experience too. You may well cry. That's okay. There's a well of suppressed tears within us all, I think, and it's healing to have them come out.

You may find that you can't hold your own gaze for very long at all—that's okay too. Do what you can, and you can increase the length the next time. This is you truly seeing you, and honoring you and being with yourself, and that's a big step.

So, only hold your own gaze for as long as you can. If you cry, though, keep tapping until the tears ease and dry up and the upset is gone. The tapping will process the emotions that cause the tears and will move them on; it's important to do that rather than let the emotions just hang around or, even worse, get repressed again.

If you can do this every day, for even three to five minutes, you will find it very healing. You will learn to be with yourself, to know yourself, to acknowledge yourself, to fully see yourself. This is powerful because, as part of the narcissistic upbringing, we were never allowed to fully acknowledge ourselves. Our narcissistic mother wanted all the attention on herself, of course, so we had to be outward-focusing toward her, rather than inward-focusing on ourselves. This exercise is to counterbalance that.

Also, given the toxic shame and the sense of being born broken that we have spoken of before, it's a huge step, and so healing, to just accept ourselves fully and unconditionally.

Hugs,
Danu

BE SELFISH!

Dear DONM,

One of the things that narcissistic mothers teach us is that only her feelings matter. Our feelings are to be discounted by her and/or used against us as proof of our failure and faults. And we're taught to discount those feelings ourselves.

Only her desires matter. Ours are to be ignored by both her and us, or used as weapons against us because the more we want something, the more she can hurt us by denying it or breaking it or taking it away.

And so we learn, growing up, to discount all that is important to us. To put ourselves last, if at all.

This is made worse by society's messages to women about being selfless givers. We hear that message in the very air we breathe. It seeps into our pores and fills our lungs, and we absorb that belief until it's very much part of us.

Also, we can loathe so much what our narcissistic mother is that we want to do the opposite of her in everything we can. So if she is selfish, we'll be selfless.

And so, it might have been hard to read the title of this chapter: "Be selfish!" Did it trigger stress for you? I wouldn't be surprised if it did, as it is so challenging to the rules we were taught to live by.

But this DONM journey is one of examining our beliefs, isn't it? Holding them up to the light and seeing if they're true or just part of the dysfunction. I offer you the possibility of looking again at this belief. I offer you the suggestion that it's okay to be selfish. Indeed, even more radically, that it's essential to be selfish.

Being selfish gets bad press, but I'd like us to reclaim that word. I'm not talking about being self-centered or self-absorbed or anything like that. Instead, I am speaking of being appropriately selfish. You don't leave your child hungry because you're too busy with your hobby to cook dinner. That's narcissistically selfish, and of course we're not talking about that. But we DONMs can tend to be so far to the other end of that spectrum that we're falling off the edge.

For all the reasons shared above, we often stop looking after ourselves enough. We fail to be appropriately selfish. And that's what I offer you here—the prospect, the possibility of coming back to balance, of being appropriately selfish. Of taking time in the day to do something fun for you, of spending some money on you, of saying no to things that don't serve you. It's part of putting good boundaries in place, in a way. You can't put in place good boundaries unless you know you deserve to have boundaries—unless, to phrase it another way, you are selfish enough to do so.

If it feels too difficult to be selfish, if every part of you clenches in stress at the thought—that is because she taught you well to put yourself last. As ever, I recommend EFT to shift that basic belief.

All best for now, and keep going on your wonderful healing journey!

Hugs,
Danu

CAN YOU GO NO CONTACT WITH HER APPROVAL?

Dear DONM,

I've had many DONMs write to me and ask me when it's okay to go no contact, and how to have their narcissistic mother realize that it's justified. What horrible deed of the narcissistic mother is enough that even she (the narcissistic mother herself) will realize and accept her daughter's departure and not blame her for leaving?

Well, of course I don't know every narcissistic mother. But I would hazard a guess that there is no such deed and that this will never happen. One of the defining traits of a narcissist, don't forget, is that they are never wrong. And I mean *never*, literally. Not "rarely." But never.

Hell could be an ice-block and pigs could be free-wheeling merrily over our heads, and a narcissistic mother would still be pouting or shouting or weeping that she *didn't* do it, and you're misremembering due to your vivid imagination, and it wasn't her fault anyway because you made her do it, and you're oversensitive to be getting upset about it, and you're so mean to be so nasty to her when she's just a poor little old lady/has a bad cold/insert drama of choice here.

So, she won't ever acknowledge that you're justified in cutting off contact. But, you know, that doesn't matter. Or, more accurately, it only matters to the extent that we let it matter.

No, we won't be able to leave with her blessing and her acceptance and her understanding. But we are the ones who put that condition on it (for good and understandable reasons, don't get me wrong), and we can remove that condition if we choose.

Okay, that condition might well be ingrained and tough to remove (cough *EFT* cough!), but it is still a rule that we have somehow come to believe, and we can change it and remove it. And therein lies our freedom. Yes, if we cut off contact, she'll have her narrative about that and will rant or weep (depending on what she thinks will get most traction in that moment) to whoever will listen about her ungrateful daughter, or her delusional daughter, or whatever story she's telling.

You can't prevent that. There's no mileage in even trying. But you can stop it preventing *you* from making the right choices for you.

You can free yourself from the need for her approval. You won't get it, ever (except temporarily and conditionally, as bait and manipulation). But freedom lies in accepting that fact and not trying any longer. If it's right for you to go no contact, then you can make that decision for you.

Hugs,
Danu

NARCISSISTS' NO-WIN SITUATIONS

Dear DONM,

Narcissists, especially those toward the more malignant end of the spectrum, often delight in creating no-win situations to tie us up in knots. No matter what we do, we're in the wrong, and they manage to get drama out of it.

So, for example, they might want to organize a trip to the movies. So they check what's playing and say, "Would you prefer Film A or Film B?" You say, "Film A, please." And then you get a whole discussion, designed to wear you down, about how Film B is actually much better and got better reviews, etc., etc., until you agree to see Film B.

But . . . !

If you had said Film B, then most likely the reverse would have happened. Suddenly Film A is the best film ever and is the unmissable one.

We can never know for a fact if that would happen as we can't go back in time to test both options. But the fact that you never happen to pick the right film would be the clue.

So, you might get clever and say, "Oh, I don't care. They both sound good. Let's go to whichever one you prefer." But no. That's too easy and too drama-free and too normal and sensible. If you did that, you would get "Oh, I'm so sick and tired of this! I'm trying to organize a nice evening out for us, and you won't even engage enough to show any interest in which film we go to. I'm tired of doing all the work here and making all the effort."

Or you might get "God, you're such a nonperson, aren't you, never having any opinions. No wonder everyone thinks you're so boring," etc. The script will no doubt change. But the underlying theme, that they'll maneuver things so that you're always in the wrong, remains.

Gotta love these narcissists, right? And by "love" I do, of course, mean hate, loathe, and despise.

Hugs,
Danu

ROOTS AND WINGS

Dear DONM,

They say good parents give their children both roots and wings. Narcissists, of course, give their children neither.

I think of my own situation. I have no place I can really call my hometown. In itself I don't mind that too much, as some people do move a lot, and that is not necessarily part of narcissistic abuse.

But what is part of the narcissistic dynamic is the fact that I have no roots to any family. We had no relationship with any aunts, uncles, or cousins growing up. They all had relationships with each other, and we were the family left out in the cold, and I could never understand it. Now of course I understand it fully. The result was that when I grew into adulthood, I didn't know anyone in my extended family. (In the last few years I have gotten in touch with a few cousins, and that is wonderful. But those relationships are new and fragile as yet, until we get to know each other better.)

So there are no roots. I often feel unanchored. I have found my own home, with some success, but it never replaces that hole at the base of it all.

As for wings—ha!

When I look back on how woefully I was prepared for adult life, I am aghast. Between my parents and my educators, I was given no direction, no support, no encouragement. I launched into adult life clumsily, and I was vulnerable. You don't know what you don't know, and it took me years to even figure out what the gaps were.

Rather than having roots and wings, children of narcissists are like tumbleweed.

Slowly I have realized the gaps, and equally slowly I have worked to fill them (education, financial management, self-care, etc.). But I am doing at fifty what most people do in their mid-twenties, and those missing years will never be filled. I write this, not to whine or complain, but because I know this is the reality for us all. The details may differ between our different situations, but the broad picture remains the same: no one raised by a narcissist has either roots or wings. To provide these things requires mature and unselfish parenting, and that, we definitely did not get.

I don't have any solution to offer; I'm still trying to figure it all out myself. But I did want to acknowledge this reality for us all.

Hugs,
Danu

WHAT ABOUT THERAPY
WITH YOUR MOTHER?

Dear DONM,

As you know, daughters of narcissistic mothers expend hours and days and years of time, and infinite amounts of effort and energy, trying to fix their relationship with their mothers. You have, no doubt, been there, done that.

This is because until we learn about narcissistic personality disorder and fully accept its implications, either we believe her lies that we're the problem or, even if we don't, we still cling to the hope that the situation is fixable.

I emphasize that knowing about NPD isn't enough—you need to also fully accept its implications, which are that she will not change, that she does not want to improve things (except on her terms, which means your complete surrender).

But allowing ourselves to fully acknowledge exactly what NPD means is very hard. I know that. And until you're able to take the step of full acceptance, you might well still be trying to fix your relationship with her. As part of that quest, you might suggest she come to counseling with you. Or she might even be the one who suggests therapy, and that can give you hope and make you think that, yes, there is a chance this can be fixed.

However, therapy with a narcissistic mother never ends well. As I remember, the experience of every single member of the forum I ran who went to therapy/counseling with their mothers was a terrible one.

This is because, most often, the narcissistic mother picked the therapist or it was one she was going to already. This meant that the therapist was already on the narcissistic mother's side—especially so if it was her current therapist, as that therapist had already heard whole sagas about what a bad daughter she had, how much trouble the daughter caused, how nothing pleased her, etc.

The situation is further compounded by the fact that the narcissistic mother, on the one hand, and her daughter, on the other, had very different agendas about going to therapy. The daughter would be entering into it in a spirit of genuine exploration, trying to fix the relationship, to come to a better understanding, etc. The mother would be doing it in order to get the therapist to fix the daughter so she'd be more amenable and cooperative. In this scenario, the mother and therapist would gang up on the daughter and make her doubly convinced she was the problem, a terrible person, etc.

I'm not saying that in this case the therapist would be deliberately ganging up on the daughter (although she might be; therapists can be narcissists too). But therapists are only human, and they can be fooled by clever narcissists, and that's why it would be happening. I'll go as far as to say that if this is an ongoing, regular therapist of your mother's, then it's guaranteed, for reasons I explain below, that that therapist will have swallowed the Kool-Aid and will believe your mother's lies and that your mother is the poor innocent victim. No matter how innocent the intentions of the therapist, though, the result will be the same: you being abused further.

The other possibility is that you go to your therapist, who is forewarned about your mother's NPD (and I do sincerely hope that if you have a therapist, she fully supports you and understands about

NPD). Or it might be a therapist new to you both, who is knowledge-able enough to identify your mother's narcissism.

And if the therapist does call your mother on her behavior, what will happen then, guaranteed, is that your mother will find some way to stop going. She'll declare the therapist a quack who doesn't know what they're talking about, or she'll declare that her going to therapy is a waste of time when it's you who's the problem, or she'll suddenly come down with some illness that stops her from going or with financial woes that mean she can't afford it (although that illness and those financial woes won't stop her from doing other things).

That is why, if your mother has an ongoing therapist, that thera-pist is guaranteed to have been fooled by her—because the very fact that your mother is still going means she's hearing only what she wants to hear from that therapist. So, you'll see why therapy with your narcissistic mother isn't going to work as intended.

Having said all that, there can be reasons why you'd want to agree to therapy together. For example, one very valid reason is that you want to know you have done absolutely all you can to sort out this relationship before you walk away.

If you do decide to do this, here are a few suggestions:

Make sure *you* pick the therapist, rather than letting your mother do it. Even better if it's your therapist to start with (although you may then be sure your mother will accuse that therapist of being on your side and ganging up on her when the therapist calls her on any of her behavior).

When you speak to the therapist beforehand, ask them what they know about NPD, and get them to tell you what they know rather than you asking direct questions.

You can say, "I'm interested in coming to work with you with my mother. We're having issues that I believe involve narcissistic personality disorder. Do you know much about that?"

And if they say, "Yes, I do," you can ask, "Could you share with me some of your understandings about it?" and then let them speak.

Only pick a therapist who has accurate information about NPD. You'd be surprised and shocked at how many therapists do not know. If they balk at being asked questions like this, then they're not the therapist for you anyway.

If you find a good therapist who does know about NPD, you and your mother can go there. The outcome will be that your mother throws some kind of hissy fit, storms out, and refuses to go back—but you will have gotten the result of knowing you tried all that you could.

Hugs,
Danu

FALSE DOORS AND STONE WALLS

Dear DONM,

One of the challenges of being a DONM is not only that you have to learn about narcissistic personality disorder, but you also have to accept its implications fully; in other words, you have to accept the truth that your narcissistic mother never loved you, never can love you, and never will love you—and that that's no reflection on your own worth whatsoever. It's about her being emotionally crippled so that she just doesn't have it in her to love anyone but herself.

As an aside, sometimes, from a safe distance, I can find myself feeling somewhat sorry for narcissists, who miss out on the joy of loving others. Love makes our world vibrant and full of color, and here they are living in a kind of gray-sepia flat world without that.

But then I recall just how much devastation and hurt and misery they cause, and my sympathy dissolves. But anyway.

Until we realize this truth about our mothers, we can spend years and decades of our one precious life knocking on a door that will never ever open. It's not even a door; it's a solid wall painted to look like a door. Or maybe a solid wall that doesn't even look much like a door (because sometimes narcissistic mothers don't even bother to pretend very hard), but our own understandable desire and society's expectations of what a mother is convince us it's a door.

But no matter how well or badly it's painted, it's not a door; it's solid rock. And solid rock can never swing open.

Freedom lies in accepting this fact, no matter how painful. You can use EFT by yourself to make those shifts, or just make the decision in some other way. By deciding to, maybe. This perhaps sounds flippant but it's not. Your freedom is just a thought away.

And once you've made the decision, then what? There may well be grief as you process this (and EFT will help with that too; just tap as you are feeling the grief). But after that, there is freedom.

I invite you to see the possibilities in this. The fact is that the endless futile knocking on that stone wall took so much of your energy and attention. It was exhausting, wasn't it? And now you don't have to do that anymore!

Think of all that you can do, and be, and have, once that energy is freed up! You have been working so very hard on a useless task, and now you can (after a rest) use that energy and power for your own purposes.

You can redefine yourself too. You can find out who you really are now that you know you're not your mother's unlovable child. I repeat, you are not who she said you were. She held up a false mirror to you, to show you a grotesque caricature of yourself, because that kept you weak and trapped. But you are not who she said you were.

One small but effective step I recommend is to tap (i.e., use EFT on) the affirmation "I am not who she said I am," over and over for a few weeks until that shift happens and you know the truth of it. You don't have to spend hours doing it, but try to incorporate it into your life—five minutes three times a day perhaps. And when you're standing waiting for a kettle to boil, or hanging around at the front door waiting for someone to finally be ready to leave—in other words, in those spare moments we all have—tap each point in turn, saying on each one: "I am not who she said I am."

This process is incredibly freeing and empowering, as you will find.

Hugs,
Danu

"ARE YOU STILL GOING ON ABOUT THAT?"

Dear DONM,

One trait of emotional abusers, including narcissists, is that they a) do not want to resolve anything, and b) don't want you to insist on them resolving anything. And so they operate a Magical Cosmic Reset Button, which means that after a certain amount of time has passed, they don't have to discuss a previous problem or situation. The slate is wiped clean.

This, of course, means they never have to acknowledge what they did and, more importantly, they never have to change their behavior in order to make sure they don't do the same thing again.

The only problem with this wonderful system comes when you start trying to mess with it and hold them accountable, and their go-to line to stop you in that attempt is: "Oh, you're not *still* going on about that?"

The word *still* means that you've been holding onto it far too long. You're bearing grudges. You never let things go. You never forgive and forget. You're so unreasonable.

Or they might place the emphasis a bit differently and say, "Oh, you're not still going on about *that*, are you?" The word *that* shows how trivial the incident was, and here you are, blowing it up into a huge issue. It was a nothing, a moment, a minor thing, but no, you have to go on and on and on about it, don't you? You have to make a federal case out of it. You're so unreasonable.

And on the face of it, what they say sounds plausible. After all, we know it's not adult or mature to bear grudges or to take offense at every tiny thing. But you know that what they're saying is not plausible. Don't fall for it.

With regard to the length of time since the incident happened, the fact is that an incident is not resolved until it's *resolved*. Something like that is not a flesh wound that heals itself with time. It's a tear in fabric that needs mending and will stay torn until that happens, and perhaps will even fray more in the meantime.

It is entirely reasonable to have a conversation like this: "I didn't like the way x situation happened. Can we talk about it and find a solution going forward that meets both our needs?"

As for their second ploy, implying that the situation was trivial, my thoughts are that it doesn't matter if it's trivial (as long as you're not being pathologically controlling). If it's important to you, it's important in the relationship and should be open for discussion. In a healthy relationship, these things can be discussed with an open mind on each person's part, and a good solution or compromise can be found. Sometimes the solution is that they explain their position and you accept it once you realize their side of it, rather than them changing their behavior.

So, say you tell a friend, "I don't like it when you don't text to say you're safe once you've gotten home," and they say, "I hate feeling I have to text you. We've said our goodbyes and to me that's enough." Well, the solution might be either that they text in future, or that you accept that they don't text when you realize how big a deal it is for them. In a way it doesn't matter what the actual solution is; the important thing is the respectful and caring discussion about it.

But my guess is that if you're psyching yourself up to bring up a topic with your narcissistic mother, it's not trivial at all. You let the trivial things go because they're not worth the trouble. These are big and important things to you. So don't fall into her trap of believing that because she deems it trivial, you have to let it go. As I already said, even if it was trivial, it'd be fair to discuss it, and it's not trivial anyway.

So don't believe her when she does whatever her preferred variation is of "Oh, you're not still going on about that are you?"

Having said all this, though, the reality is that narcissists will never be held accountable for their actions and will never agree to discuss it. If you try to insist, they'll block you another way. My own mother would snap, "That's enough, Danu!" and that was usually enough to stop me cold. And on the rare occasions that it didn't work, when I, heart thudding and stomach churning, would persist in something important to me, she'd collapse in tears and deflect it that way.

So, none of what I'm saying here is about finding a way to get through to your narcissistic mother and make her understand your position. There is no such way to find.

It's about your own awareness, though. It's about you recognizing that you are not holding grudges or getting upset about trivial things, no matter how much she tries to spin it that way. It's about you seeing it for the manipulation it is, rather than believing her.

Hugs,
Danu

GIVING YOURSELF PERMISSION

Dear DONM,

Our society is based on a hierarchical model where so many people get to be the boss of us. That was true when we were children, for sure, from parents to teachers to even random adults. In a healthy model the reins of authority are handed over to us when we are old enough.

Even so, I think many people are still looking for authority to tell them something is okay to do. It seems to me that in their fear they're looking for somebody in charge to say, "It's okay to start your own business/write your novel/go traveling around the world."

How much more does this apply to DONMs who have experienced nothing but the misuse of authority?

I get a lot of emails from DONMs asking me, in effect, if it is okay to go no contact with their narcissistic mothers. I understand that entirely: for years and years I kept in contact with my parents despite hating every minute of it and being emotionally bruised after every encounter, because I thought I had to. I didn't realize I was allowed to not be in touch with my parents. If I'd had anyone to ask for permission, I sure as hell would have done it too.

I make a point, of course, to never give permission as such, as that's absolutely not my place. But I try to say to these DONMs that they can give themselves permission, that they're allowed to do that, that they're the boss of their own lives—and that's what I want to say to you too. And maybe to myself as well, as I need constant reminding!

I have realized that one of the hugely empowering things in your life, with regard to your narcissistic mother and everything else—is to give yourself permission. For example, no one gave me permission to set up the DONM website. I just did it. And any of you can do the same. Also, I'm a novelist of sorts. When I had my first novel published a good few years ago, I was amazed at the number of people who said, "Don't you have to have a degree in English to write a novel?" In other words, did I not need permission/validation from authorities such as a university to do this? Nope. I just wrote it.

There's security in having permission, I think, that you don't have when you do stuff yourself. Someone else has said it's okay. But in so many things in life, there is no one who's authorized to say it's okay, so you could be waiting forever.

I'd like to offer you the possibility of thinking about what you might do in your life if you had the sense of being allowed to do it, and then giving yourself that sense. It might sound crazy, but just try it—speak it aloud. Say: "I, [your name], hereby give myself full and absolute permission to do x." (I'm sure it goes without saying that this only applies to things that are ethical.)

Be aware of the sensations in your body as you say this. Do you feel a tension when you do? This shows that you don't really believe in your own permission. Which is fully understandable for all the reasons shared above.

If this is the case, you can just plow on regardless, ignoring the sensations, and when your body realizes it's not dangerous to do this, it'll feel better. Or use EFT to erase the fears and doubts. When we follow our dreams, we fulfill our own lives and souls, but I think we also add to the world. As Marianne Williamson says in her book *A Return to Love*, when we play big, we give others permission to do the same. So it's a win-win.

So go on: give yourself all the permission you need!

Hugs,
Danu

WHAT DOES IT MEAN?

Dear DONM,

One thing I've learned is that humans are meaning-creating creatures. This is how we see images in clouds, for example.

We don't just look at something and accept it. We instead ask what it means, and more, we decide what it means. The problem with this is twofold: the first is that we can very likely be wrong about what it means, and the second is that we do this so quickly and intuitively and subconsciously that we don't even realize we're doing it. And all that means we never get to question these decisions or judge them to see if they're right.

So, if our mother is distant and abrupt and unloving when we're small, subconsciously we conclude that it's because we're unlovable (rather than that she is incapable of loving anyone). And that becomes part of our map of our reality and impacts us for our whole lives.

So one essential step on the road to healing is to look at the meanings we put on things. This is easier said than done, as the meanings happen instantly. It takes vigilance to catch them and question them. I'm far from good at this myself. I share it because I know it's so good to do, not because I'm an expert at it. But any false meaning caught and deflected is better than none, so it's well worth the effort.

And so, if a friend doesn't return your call or text quickly, you might immediately conclude that she's cross with you. An equally valid interpretation (since you don't know the facts) is that she's busy, or that her phone battery died.

I think we DONMs are too quick to assume the bad interpretation of everything. It's totally understandable, of course, but it still doesn't do us any favors. The more we can catch ourselves doing that and stop it, the better.

One good exercise is to write down the fact of what happened. For example: My friend didn't call me back. And then add, "which means . . ." and freewrite what you think it means ("she's cross with me"). And then add, "which means . . ." and freewrite that next thing. You might end up with something like, "which means she won't want to be friends with me anymore." Continue this process, applying the meaning to every stage: "which means that I will be friendless and that I'm impossible to get along with and that no one wants to be friends with me."

This isn't a fun exercise, I know. But it's just bringing up to the light the stuff that's going on anyway for you beneath your awareness. No wonder you feel so stressed and upset when she doesn't call you back.

So then, when you're finished, look at your final disaster-thinking. You can use EFT on that statement if you wish to nullify it and make it lose its power, but even without that, look at it and realize how untrue it is. You have built the proverbial mountain out of the molehill. (Again, I do this too, all the time . . .)

Recognizing the games your brain is playing on you with all this can really help you to neutralize it. Because even if it's true that your friend is cross with you, it doesn't follow that she'll want to stop being friends with you. And even if *that* is true, it doesn't follow that *no one* ever wants to be friends with you.

And if, perhaps, *that* is true, well, better to know it than not, and in this case you have identified the real problem, and that is when you could perhaps look into therapy to find out why.

But I bet you'll find that your end-of-the-line disaster-thinking is so untrue as to be absurd, and that will help you realize that the meaning you put on things doesn't always serve you.

Hugs,
Danu

HELPING YOUR INNER CHILD

Dear DONM,

When I was twelve, I went through the ceremony of confirmation in the religion I was raised in. I am sharing this with you not because of the exact occasion but because it was an occasion that was supposed to be about me. Because I thought it would be a time when they'd make a bit of a fuss over me, a time when I'd be a bit special to them for once.

That morning, all was chaos as my mother tried to organize us all. There were three children younger than me, including an eight-month-old baby, so I can see the pressures. But my father was there, and my younger brother was ten, so surely able to help a bit.

My mother needed something from the store about fifteen minutes' walk away, and she ordered me to go and get it. I recall the shock I felt. This was my special day! Surely I couldn't just be sent on an errand like it was an ordinary day. I didn't think of it until afterward, but why couldn't my father or brother have gone? I did try to protest that I shouldn't have to go on this day of all days, and she yelled at me and I caved immediately, as ever. It wasn't that I objected to going to the store or helping out. But to be ordered to do so like this, with absolutely no mention or consideration that it was my special day, really hurt. If she'd spoken to me gently and nicely, and had said, "Danu, I know it's your special day, and I'm so sorry to ask you, but would you be able to go down to the store for me?" then it would have been very different. But of course she didn't do that.

There was, as usual, no softness or gentleness or understanding. To add insult to injury, we only had one hairbrush for the whole household (which is bizarre in itself, as I think of it), and I couldn't find it, so I had to go with my wild thick hair unbrushed and messy.

I can still recall twelve-year-old me walking to the store, shoulders slumped, upset, confused, burning with the injustice of it, hurting at yet again realizing that I didn't matter, I wasn't important to them at all, that they were just going through the motions of parenting—doing the confirmation thing because that was what you did. It certainly wasn't about me in any way. But as I recalled this experience, I did something different.

In my imagination, I, the Danu of today, stepped into the scene. I walked up to twelve-year-old Danu and fell into step beside her. "Hey," I said to her.

She looked up in surprise at someone arriving beside her out of nowhere.

"I'm you in forty years' time," I told her. "The grown-up you."

She didn't freak out or run away or anything. This being my imagination and my story, she reacted as I needed her to: calmly, as if it was totally reasonable for a time-traveler from the future to come back to chat with her. She was instead curious and interested in what I had to say.

And what I had to say was this: "Danu, you need to know that this is no reflection on you or your value as a human being. Yes, the message is that you are so valueless that even your special days are nothing to them. But it's a wrong message. It's a false message. It's about a flaw in them, not in you."

I spoke urgently, as this was essential information for her to know: "You are a wonderful, valuable human, just as everyone else is. You are not less-than. They are giving you false information. Yes, you have to endure the day as they create it, but you don't have to believe the subtext about your value. Okay?"

She brightened. Her shoulders straightened a bit and she stood taller. "I understand," she said. "Thanks for that." And she walked off toward the store, and I stood and watched her go, happy that she felt better about it.

Well, that's ridiculous, you might say. That was just all in your imagination. For sure. Of course it was. But the thing is that the hurting twelve-year-old Danu was only in my imagination too. The real twelve-year-old Danu is long gone.

The scar and hurt are in the present, and they live in my imagination and my mind, so I can do things in the present and in my imagination/mind to heal them. Now when I think of that situation it doesn't hurt anymore. I've rewritten history. Okay, not real history. But history in the only place it exists—my mind. Now when I think of that day, I see twelve-year-old Danu being very aware of what's going on, and it helping her immeasurably.

Could you try this yourself for upsetting memories? Using due caution, of course; use your judgment on whether it's safe for you or not. If it's a very bad memory that really cannot be perceived in any different way—such as abuse—well, then you can tell her that it wasn't her fault, and that she does (you do) survive it. And you can be the loving adult helping her through it. If it's too triggering for you to be there while she's experiencing it, you can go to her after an incident. I'd love to hear how this goes for you.

There's a way of using EFT to help even more with this memory work, and I'll talk more about that next.

Hugs,
Danu

USING EFT WITH YOUR INNER CHILD

Dear DONM,

I know that heading might feel very weird and New-Agey. But you can think of your inner child as just the memories in your current brain, as we shared in the previous letter. And EFT is, well, yeah, it is a little bit New-Agey, but it works even so.

To use EFT for your memories, you go and visit the younger you in your memory, as I shared in the last letter. If it's a different younger you than you met before, introduce yourself to her again. She is, in some very real way, a different person from the previous memory.

And this time you tell her you have a way of making her feel better, and would it be okay with her if you tried it? (You always respect her boundaries like this.) If she says no, accept it fully, and ask her if she would like you to stay and talk with her, or hold her hand, etc. Do whatever she's comfortable with.

You might find that after a while she asks you what your method of making her feel better is, once you're not pressuring her. But if she never does, so be it. Try it on another memory another time.

When you find a younger you who is willing, what you do is this: If she is already upset about what happened, just sit beside her and visualize/imagine yourself tapping on her. Tap on all the points in order. Keep tapping just as if she were a real person until the stress leaves her and she's calm about it.

Or ask her to tell you what happened, and tap on her while she tells you.

At the end, you can offer her a better outcome. You can say, "Instead of you being here in your room crying after what Mom said to you, would you like to go somewhere nice? We can go any-where you like." If she says yes, then ask her where she'd like to go, emphasizing that she can go wherever her imagination chooses: a beach, a fairground, the moon—anywhere! And once she chooses, in your imagination bring her there and be with her for a while there. And when it's time for you to come back into the real world, ask her who she'd like to come and be with her there—a friend maybe, or an animal. Conjure up that image when she asks, and you can leave her there, safe and happy.

You will find this exercise incredibly powerful and helpful for you—the you of today—as, of course, it changes your memories too.

I urge you not to dismiss this suggestion as being too weird, as it really is powerful for healing.

Hugs,
Danu

IT'S JUST SMOKE AND MIRRORS AND CURTAINS

Dear DONM,

Do you remember that iconic scene in *The Wizard of Oz* where they pull back the curtain to reveal that the wizard is just a pathetic little man operating levers? That image comes to me often when I think of narcissistic mothers, because they are like that.

Assuming she does not have a financial hold over you (which is very possible; they're good at manipulating situations like that), and that she is not violent toward you (and if she is, please, please know you don't have to accept that and you have options there too), her power is all smoke and mirrors and curtains.

Her power is only words, in other words. And her words only have the impact we give them. It's totally understandable that we give them huge impact, as we've been trained to do since birth, but what I am sharing with you now is the possibility that you break that pattern.

This goes back to the boundaries that we spoke of before. Know that you have the power to put boundaries in place, and there's probably (depending on your specific situation) nothing she can do about that.

The example I share applies to my father rather than my mother. My mother never showed any interest in me (beyond a vague "How are things with you?"; then she would interrupt my answer as soon as whatever I said triggered some thought of her own), so I never had to worry about that with her. However, my father showed great interest in my life and would ask about specifics. This might sound great, but it used to make me so stressed when he did it, and it took me ages to figure out why.

I finally figured it out: he would ask questions about a situation until he could find, or assume, something bad about it and then commiserate about that, having fully burst my bubble. I bet if I told him I won the lottery, he'd say mildly, "Oh, well done. Do they send you a check?" and when I'd say, "No, you have to go up to their headquarters to collect it," he'd commiserate sadly, "Oh, that's awful; what a hassle."

So, yes. Once I realized this, I determined to never tell him anything important again. And once I had managed to pluck up my courage to actually follow through on my determination (and that took a while, for sure), the next time he asked about a big project of mine, I said, "I don't want to talk about that project anymore." He said in the dangerous voice he used if he was being thwarted, "And why don't you want to talk about it anymore?"

I kept my voice calm, even though my heart was racing, and said lightly, "I don't want to talk about why I don't want to talk about it."

His face was quite a sight! Fury for sure, but frustration too because he had lost. He realized we could go on endlessly if he pursued it: "I don't want to talk about why I don't want to talk about why I don't want to talk about it anymore," and so on.

And that was the day I realized no one can make you be part of a conversation you don't want to be part of; the day I realized they don't get to be the deciders of what I have to share and discuss. It was very empowering and freeing, and I want to share that with you too.

Hugs,
Danu

HOW A CYCLING HINT
HAS HELPED ME WITH LIFE

Dear DONM,

I'm an avid cyclist. Not a very fit or hardcore cyclist, mind you, but an enthusiastic one. One thing I struggle with is hills. I read a hint on a cycling forum that, when you're cycling up a difficult hill, you should keep your eyes on the ground in front of you (as much as is compatible with safety, of course, glancing ahead every so often to check). Keeping your gaze close rather than looking way ahead will help, they said.

Well, I tried it and it totally does help. They didn't know why, and I'm not sure either, but I think it's because it breaks the task into tiny, manageable bits. Instead of seeing the huge hard hill ahead of you, you are only focusing on this tiny bit of it.

I think this is a good metaphor for life, whenever you reach metaphorical hills. And let's face it, DONMs have more than our fair share of metaphorical hills, don't we?

So I suggest that when all is too difficult, just take baby steps. Do the tiniest little thing you are able to do. It doesn't even matter if it's the right thing. It is movement, and when you're stuck, movement in any direction will give you much-needed momentum. So do the one tiny thing you can, focusing on the immediate surroundings (still metaphorically speaking).

If you look up and try to make a big-picture plan, it can be overwhelming and you don't know where to go and what to do, so you stay stuck. (Obviously, if you're in a position to look at the big picture and make a strategic plan, then do that. This is advice for when that's not possible for you.)

And so, take baby steps, and keep taking baby steps for as long as you have to, until you are far enough away from the original blockage (I am mixing my metaphors dreadfully here, I know!) and can then look around you. And yes, you might be far from where you should be going, but you can go from the new place to the correct destination then, when you have more momentum and less panicked paralysis.

Hugs,
Danu

SOMETIMES IT REALLY IS ABOUT YOU!

Dear DONM,

I spoke before about how it's not narcissistic to want it to be about you. I know that can be hard for DONMs to realize because we were taught so hard that it is never ever, ever about us. But that is a message that has to be handed back, I think. Because sometimes it really is about you.

This was brought home to me very strongly some time ago. A friend of mine was due to have her first baby. Now, we don't have the custom of baby showers where I live, so normally there is no official celebration of women in her situation.

But she wanted to acknowledge this special occasion, so she organized a women's night, with conversation and poems and dancing, and good wishes for her. I was so impressed with the way she did this, claiming her right to have this special occasion for herself and arranging it accordingly.

Even more so, when, during the evening, we were dancing and she put herself in the middle of the circle, so that we were dancing around her. She was very clearly and deliberately making herself the center of the whole evening. And this is a woman who is in no way narcissistic, let me stress. She is kind and warm and gentle and compassionate and equally ready to make others' occasions be about them, which is why it was such a powerful lesson to me: you clearly don't have to be narcissistic to make it about you.

I think that many DONMs, including me, have trouble with that concept, as all we ever experienced was narcissistic attention-seeking.

So to see this woman, with such grace, make it appropriately about her was so good for me. I learned that it's okay to make it about me when it's appropriate. And I would love if you could learn this secondhand from her example. Because, sometimes it really is about you. It really is.

What things do you think are appropriately about you? Maybe you could make a list. In this way you are consciously naming and claiming these things. Here are some suggestions: Your birthday. Your wedding (that's about you and your spouse). Your graduation. Your baby shower. Your bereavement. Your miscarriage.

And, I suggest, you need have no shame about wanting to make those about you, about you being the center of attention then. You need have no shame about protecting those occasions from being hijacked by your mother.

Hugs,
Danu

WHEN SOMEONE SAYS THEY LOVE YOU, IT SHOULD FEEL LIKE THEY DO

Dear DONM,

Narcissistic mothers are, in my experience, very good at saying "I love you." But they don't act like they love us; far from it.

This is one of the many forms of the narcissistic abuse called gaslighting. *Gaslighting* refers to the way narcissists and other abusers rewrite history in their favor, and lie to us about reality to the extent that we doubt our own perceptions in the face of their insistence.

Because we are trained to believe her version of reality above our own, we can end up believing she loves us even though, truly, it doesn't feel like that.

Or we begin to think that narcissistic abuse is what love really is, is what love feels like. Of course we do. How can we not, when it's our main, or only, experience? And of course this sets us up for future abuse as we accept the same behavior from others who say they love us.

So they tell us they love us even as they demean us and intimidate us and dismiss us and invalidate us and gaslight us and undermine us and sabotage us . . . and we still believe them.

It can take a long time to realize what love feels like, and even longer to insist upon it from those who say it.

These are my thoughts on what healthy love feels like. They actually apply to all relationships, I think. They apply to those who say (either implicitly or in as many words) "I am your friend" as much as they apply to those who say they love us.

Love feels respectful. It does, indeed, as St. Paul is quoted as saying in the Bible, feel "patient and kind."

People who love you can disagree with you, and even criticize you, but will do so mostly in a respectful, patient, and kind way. I say "mostly" because anyone can be impatient and lose their temper once in a while, but it should very much be the exception and not the rule. In healthy relationships, they should apologize afterward. I think that even when healthy people lose their tempers, they still don't get abusive. They might yell, "I am sick and tired of the way you do x, y, z," but they don't yell abuse at you, telling you what a horrible person you are to do x, y, z.

You can relax, knowing that you are safe. I think this is a good measure: Check in with your feelings around this person. Are you serene and calm and relaxed about being with them? Or is there a bit of tension and nervousness? Do you have to feel alert? This is a good indicator, as your feelings will not lie to you, even though your poor brainwashed brain might.

Those who truly love you encourage you and support you in your endeavors. They do not undermine you. This can be a subtle one, as abusers can cleverly undermine while seeming to support you: "Here, let me help you with that. You know you're not that good at it, and I want you to succeed in it."

Those who love you see the best image of you. They're not naïve about you: they see you clearly, faults and all. But they hold the full package in high esteem. They see more good about you than bad. (On the other hand, abusers are all about your faults and have a very poor image of you, which they are happy to share regularly with you.)

Also, those who love you respect your boundaries.

And so, one lesson I have learned is to pay attention to how people treat me and to assess our relationship based on that. Words are cheap. It is easy to say you love someone, but not so easy to act in love. The act, then, is the thing that has the value.

Words can even be weapons used against us, as manipulation. Sometimes abusers know they don't love us, but they say it to reel us in, to manipulate us. Listening instead to the actions will protect against that too. And by "actions," I mean *consistent* actions. Narcissists can act well for a while, in the "courtship" phase of a relationship. But they cannot keep it up for too long.

And what if the narcissist means it when they say "I love you"? I think my narcissistic mother genuinely believed she loved me, and she may even have had some feelings of mild fondness for me. But it was a cheap love, love that demanded nothing of her, no care or thought or kindness or empathy or even the tiniest sacrifice. That kind of love is of no use at all. It is pure self-indulgence on her behalf, giving her the warm fuzzies of saying it and even feeling it. It is her love serving her, as everything serves a narcissist. I have no need of such love. I deserve better than that.

And so, of course, do you.

Hugs,
Danu

FEELING THE FEELINGS

Dear DONM,

One thing we DONMs have in common is that we were forbidden from expressing negative feelings. In many cases we were even forbidden from feeling them. In time we hid them, even from ourselves perhaps, and certainly from the world.

I remember my mother coming home one day, all proud, because a local shopkeeper had told her, "Oh, I love to see Danu coming in. She's always so bright and cheerful that she cheers up the whole place."

And for sure, that's what I was like. Even now, if ever I was to speak with my mother about my youth she'd say, "But you were happy! You were bright and cheerful and chatty."

And that is true. Well, the bit about bright and cheerful and chatty is true. The bit about being happy? Who knows? My relationship with my own emotions was so perverted that I don't even know. I know I had depression and suicide ideation (and one genuine attempt at age sixteen) and eating disorders going on. In later years, still cheerful and outgoing and chatty, I had addictions, which I have battled until recently.

And I didn't dare express anything else. "Stop crying or I'll give you something to cry about" was a favorite statement in my house whenever I was upset. (Particularly when I was upset about her treatment of me; in fairness, I was allowed to be upset about other things.)

You might have heard phrases like "Turn that frown upside down" or "Smile!"

We DONMs ended up not even knowing what we were feeling half the time, and maybe being so repressed we didn't feel anything at all the rest of the time. It's impossible to clamp down on bad emotions without also clamping down on good ones.

Our narcissistic mother's theft of our emotions is one of her worst crimes, in my opinion. Emotions are our barometers for our lives. They're an absolutely integral part of our birthright as humans.

One of the most essential steps on this journey is to reclaim our emotions. That isn't as easy as it sounds. We're so trained to ignore them that half the time we don't even "hear" them. We're not even aware of them, or we're eating them or drinking them or smoking them or purging them or injecting them as ways of avoiding them.

Emotions can be scary. They can be overwhelming. No wonder we don't want to risk that. Here's the thing, though: emotions cannot harm us. Even the worst sadness or grief cannot harm us. It does feel uncomfortable, but that feeling is just another emotion. And remember, emotions are something you have, not something you are. All emotions are temporary.

I've mentioned it before, but the trick of observing your emotions while they're happening is a very powerful one. Let part of you be a little bit aside from what's going on, narrating it to yourself almost like a sports commentator: "The pain is in my chest, it feels like a stone, it hurts, so much grief." This helps you keep an anchor in the calm world so you don't feel like you're drowning in the emotions.

And, of course, I find EFT wonderful to use during such times. Just tap on each statement: "The pain is in my chest, it feels like a stone," etc. EFT doesn't push down the emotions; it helps process them and move them on, so it's a healthy way to deal with them.

I remember one time spending maybe an hour, maybe more, sobbing and bawling and tapping as I processed the grief around

"Who I am is not acceptable," which is the message I was taught all my life, and I know you were too.

Because that's the thing. Emotions need to be felt. They're messengers to us, and they have to be heard and then let go. None of this is about wallowing in emotions—that is equally unhealthy. But we are under no obligation anymore to bury them as our mother wanted us to.

What if you can't feel emotions at all? What if they're so repressed that they feel out of reach entirely? You can try a few things. One would be to tap on the statement "It's safe to feel my emotions." Or, conversely, if it sits better, "It's not safe to feel my emotions," and release that belief. (EFT works for both positive affirmations and for erasing the current disempowering situation.) You can try freewriting instead of, or as well as, EFT.

Also, try to remember during the day (either by yourself, or by setting alarms on your phone perhaps) to scan your body and your awareness to see how you're feeling in that moment. Feelings are held in the body, usually in a column from high in your throat down to your solar plexus. That's why emotions are called feelings, because we feel them. When you do this scan, just be aware of the feelings—you don't even have to label them for this exercise, although if you can, that's even better.

Also, check in on the following (nonexhaustive) list of emotions and ask yourself, "Do I feel this right now?" Do this when things are peaceful enough, rather than in the middle of a crisis. A crisis is no time to practice new skills.

Here is the list of emotions:

- Love

- Fear

- Surprise

- Joy

- Hurt

- Anger

- Disappointment

- Sadness

- Shame

- Disgust

- Anticipation

- Interest

- Anxiety

As you become used to feeling your emotions, you might end up feeling very negatively toward your mother, and that might trigger your desire to shut down as you're doing something strongly forbidden (e.g., thinking badly of her, which was the ultimate crime, of course).

If possible, allow yourself to feel the feelings. They are very justified. They were a long time coming. Your negative emotions about her will not hurt her directly (and, of course, I do not recommend lashing out at her), nor will she know about them by some kind of magic. I know it probably felt like that when you were small, but you are an adult now, and she has no special powers.

Once you get used to feeling your emotions, the next step is to know how to safely express them, and we'll talk about that next.

Hugs,
Danu

HOW TO EXPRESS YOUR EMOTIONS SAFELY

Dear DONM,

We spoke about getting in touch with your feelings, and now we are going to discuss how to express those feelings. These are my thoughts on the issue; as ever, take what you find useful, and leave the rest.

I think it's important to make sure not to express your feelings in a damaging way, in a way that intimidates others or hurts them. We need to make sure that our loved ones feel loved too, and that people feel safe with us.

Emotions are messengers from our body, to tell us what's going on for us. Fear tells us there may be danger about. Anger tells us someone is infringing on our rights or boundaries. Hurt tells us someone has rejected us.

Ideally, take the *message* and bring it to the person (if appropriate), rather than taking the *emotion* to them. So, if you get angry when someone is hours late, the anger is bringing it to your attention. The conversation—ideally, shared calmly—is about their lateness and the worry or disrespect you feel when that happens (or whatever is going on for you).

If you do get upset and lose your temper with them, do your best to make sure what you say isn't abusive or nasty. Use "I" statements rather than "you" statements, for example. But ideally, in a respectful relationship losing your temper should be absolutely the exception. And for sure, apologize to them afterward for the way you said it. You can absolutely still stand by *what* you said, and your right to have that issue worked out, while apologizing for *how* you approached it.

As I become aware of my emotions, I often find I am unreasonably upset about things. What I do then is to own and acknowledge the feeling, while realizing that it's unjustified. The emotions are still valid, even though their basic premise is wrong. So I feel the emotions and acknowledge them, and even share them if appropriate. I might say, "I felt angry when you went to the football game instead of spending time with me. It was inappropriate, as you are perfectly entitled to go to the game, and rationally, I am delighted you're enjoying spending time with your friends. But I was angry all the same." And even if I didn't say it to the person concerned (and I'd only do that if they were able to hear it without feeling guilty or misunderstanding me and thinking I was trying to manipulate them), the fact that I recognize and acknowledge the feelings to myself is very empowering.

EFT is very good for expressing and processing emotions. So, to continue my previous example, if I was angry about someone going to the football game, I'd tap for that emotion so I could process it and let it go. This has the twin benefit that I am acknowledging the genuine emotion (not denying it or repressing it) and letting it go painlessly, and doing all that without inflicting it on the other person.

Hugs,
Danu

ARE YOU JUST RUNNING AWAY?

Dear DONM,

A DONM wrote to me the other day asking, "But if I go no contact, is that just running away rather than staying to deal with the situation?"

It's a good question, of course. It does feel like running away, doesn't it? It can feel like a selfish, sulking, pouting, immature "I'll show her!" kind of a response. And it might be, of course. If your motivation is a sulky, immature one, then yes, I guess that would be true.

I would venture to guess, though, that that is a rare reaction. I've certainly never come across it in all these years of communicating with thousands of DONMs. Certainly, one who is asking that question, who is worrying about being like that, is not doing it. The immature one would not be second-guessing herself like this.

So, to the sincere ones (which is all of you, I have no doubt), I say this:

All the DONMs I have spoken to have considered no contact only when all else has failed. When they have tried and tried and tried to solve the situation for years and years and years. When they have sustained emotional cuts and bruises and injuries in the process of trying to connect with their mother and solve the problems in the relationship.

So, it's not a case of running away rather than staying to deal with the situation. It's running away (although I'll come back to that phrase in a minute) after having spent years trying, and failing, to deal with the situation. It's running away after years of being the only one trying to heal the situation while your mother went on gaily in her own selfish way. It's running away when you sadly, but realistically, acknowledge that the situation cannot be resolved, and certainly not by you.

And therefore, it is not running away. That is a very emotive and even self-judgmental term. It has implications of immaturity and abandoning ship at the first sign of trouble.

I would sooner say that what you are doing is calmly and realistically accepting that this situation cannot be solved, that you deserve to be free of abuse, and therefore you are removing yourself from the clutches of an abuser.

And if someone—probably you, to yourself—says, "Ah, that's ridiculous! You're just spinning it so you feel better about it," what then?

Spin is inaccurate slanting of a situation to put it in a favorable light. In this case, I believe you would be looking at the facts clearly rather than spinning. She does abuse you. You have spent years trying to sort it out. You have consistently failed. You realize now that because she's narcissistic, she cannot and will not change. You realize you deserve to be treated well and not be abused. Therefore, you have no choice but to remove yourself from the situation.

That's the reality of being the daughter of a narcissistic mother. It's not spin.

If anything, the statement that you are running away rather than dealing with the situation is spin. Negative spin, informed by the years of psychological abuse that make you see everything from her angle and nothing from your own.

So no, I don't think it's running away rather than dealing with it. I think it's calmly and appropriately walking away from an abuser.

Narcissists make it "My way or the highway," and it's reasonable to choose the highway when they are forcing such a binary choice.

Hugs,
Danu

WHAT IF YOU'RE WRONG ABOUT HER?

Dear DONM,

People often write to me and say, "But what if I'm wrong about her being narcissistic? Am I being unfair to her?"

Here's the thing: You might well be wrong. We all might be. My own mother might not be narcissistic (and wouldn't that be ironic when I literally wrote the book about it!)—it's only my best guess, after all, and a fully unqualified guess at that.

However, it seems to me that narcissistic personality disorder is a good model to work with to explain my mother's very real behaviors. Those aren't my imagination. They really happened. The toxic and dysfunctional behavior continued all my life right up until my very last encounter with her. She never tried to resolve anything in our relationship, but worked to overwhelm me and put me back into my box whenever I tried to look for better treatment. The relationship was consistently hurting me and bad for me.

So maybe there's another explanation for those things other than her being narcissistic. But you know what? It doesn't matter. It doesn't change anything in the real world. I still am entitled to protect myself from her consistently abusive behavior, regardless of what label we use for that behavior.

So I think it's not necessarily that important to know for sure if she's narcissistic. You probably will never know, in truth, as she's unlikely to ever be assessed professionally. All you can do is do your best to make sense of the messy and toxic situation, and as I say, NPD is a useful handle for it.

So my suggestion is: don't fret over it. If her behavior was bad enough that you went looking for information, then things are not right in her treatment of you, and that's the important point.

Hugs,
Danu

BUT WHAT IF SHE DOES APOLOGIZE?

Dear DONM,

One of the tenets of this narcissism thing is that they never apologize.

And so, what happens if she does actually apologize? Does it mean she's not narcissistic? Does it mean you were wrong all along and have misjudged her? Does it mean you have to forgive her and go back to where you were with her?

The thing is that narcissists are masters of what we call the "fauxpology"—the fake apology.

One classic method of doing a fauxpology is to say, "I'm sorry you were upset."

At first glance, this looks like an apology because it has the words "I'm sorry" in it, but it really isn't. It owns no fault at all. It doesn't acknowledge that she did anything wrong in the slightest. I go into more detail on this in my book *You're Not Crazy*, so I won't repeat myself here.

I wish to speak here of something I didn't say in that book: What if she does apologize better than that? A DONM wrote to me the other day with this exact query. Her mother had written to her and said, "I am sorry for all that I did wrong." This seemed to the DONM to be a full apology. It referenced what the mother did, not what the daughter might be feeling, after all.

You might feel under pressure to accept such an apology. If you don't accept such a comprehensive and full apology, aren't you now the wrong one? Aren't you the one bearing a grudge and being unfair? I don't think so.

The thing is that on the face of it, this seems like an apology. But the apology is so vague as to be useless. It's a blanket get-out-of-jail-free apology that mentions no specifics nor promises any change in behavior going forward. So it's not an apology at all. It's more manipulation.

If you want to call her bluff, either to give her every chance or to satisfy yourself that you've done all you can, you can go back to her and say something like "Thank you so much for that apology. I would like, however, for you to give me specifics of what you are apologizing for so I know what you think you did wrong and what you still think you were right about. And then we can have a discussion on how we deal with similar situations in the future."

And then wait for the explosion:

"I apologized—what more do you want? You want me to list every little thing I ever did wrong? You enjoy seeing me humiliated? You want to shame me and abuse me and make me feel awful." And so on.

The details may change, but I bet that will be the essence of it. It's not an apology. She isn't acknowledging any specific wrongdoing. She isn't making any promises to change. She is just trying to manipulate you into coming back for more abuse. You don't have to fall for it.

Hugs,
Danu

PUTTING SOMETHING
TO REST WITH NARCISSISTS

Dear DONM,

Another favorite trick of narcissists is to lightly, or even kindly, say, "Let's put this to rest and move on from here," with "this" being some disagreement you're having—no doubt, about her behavior. You may be sure that if it were *your* behavior that's in question, there would be no putting to rest suggested!

In a way, this is a first cousin to the "be a bigger person" gambit we spoke of before. The difference is that it would be the enablers who ask you to be a bigger person, and she herself who is extremely eager to put the matter to rest.

When she talks about putting something to rest and moving on, it sounds fair, right? Sounds reasonable. People do this all the time to move on from a small disagreement and carry on with their relationship. It'd be very begrudging to refuse that request. You'd be clinging to your upset and hurt most unjustly. You'd be in the wrong to do that.

That is the trap your narcissistic mother has set for you. Yes, it is reasonable in most circumstances, when it's two genuine people who care for each other and value the relationship above petty misunderstandings. Or if it's the injured party who says it, as a kind of forgiveness and letting go.

But as is the case in most things, narcissists subvert and pervert this for their own gains. They are not putting the relationship first; rather, they are trying to get away with what they've done without there being any consequences, or even acknowledgment. They're trying to get away with it without making any promises to change their behavior in the future.

They're doing their usual, in other words. They're using whatever they can in order to keep abusing you. And if you say, "Well, it'd be great to move past it, but we need to work it out first and find a better way of operating in the future," then the temper will come out and the narcissist will show her real feelings.

She wants her get-out-of-jail-free card, and she doesn't want you holding her to any standard of behavior whatsoever. This putting-the-matter-to-rest is just a ploy.

It's up to you, of course, whether you play along with it or not. But I think it might help to at least be aware of what's happening and to acknowledge to yourself that you are accepting her manipulations for the sake of peace rather than how you might be feeling now—confused and bewildered, and feeling bad about yourself for having borne a grudge or whatever the alternative to putting-to-rest is in her estimation.

In truth, though, I think that as long as you are dealing with a narcissist, trying to discuss stuff is a waste of time. If you get to the stage of putting something to rest, you've already gotten caught up in a power battle, and it's inevitably one you're going to lose.

Your only options, as I can see them, are to either suck it up or to set consequences, as we discussed before. Just as you don't have discussions with a toddler or a dog you're training—you put simple consequences in place and wait for them to learn—it's the same with narcissists.

All fun, eh?

Hugs,
Danu

DEALING WITH OTHERS'
JUDGMENT ISN'T EASY

Dear DONM,

One thing that's very hard to deal with when you're trying to free yourself from the toxicity of the narcissist is that she will, of course, smear you to everyone. She will, for sure, spin a good story, sprinkling enough truth that it sounds plausible, and people will judge you badly. Your good name will be in tatters.

The people who judge you may well be the people you care about—your extended family, family friends, the congregation at your church, and so on. They might well also be people you don't really care about—casual neighbors, your mother's hairdresser—anyone she can spin the pity story to really, as of course she's going to get lots of drama mileage about her ungrateful daughter abandoning her or being cruel to her, so lots of people will hear this.

It really, really isn't nice to be badly judged—of course it isn't. We're a social species who depend on relationships for our survival, and so good harmony is an absolute core need. In most cases, your mother cannot impact all your relationships, nor your income, etc. But we are still at heart the humans who first evolved to live interdependently in small tribes, so the fear and stress of being rejected burn deeply.

People often write to me and ask how they can avoid this, and my answer to them is this: you can't. Maybe in a few cases, with people close to both you and your mother, you can preemptively tell your story. However, if we try to tell our side of the story preemptively, we can come across as nasty and bitter. I don't know why narcissistic mothers can tell their tales and inspire pity rather than judgment—why they don't come across as nasty and bitter—but somehow, they manage it. Perhaps they play the pity card we wouldn't stoop to; perhaps they spin it as "my poor daughter, I don't know what's gotten into her." I don't really know, but I do know they manage to get more sympathetic ears than we normally can.

Telling people preemptively is fraught and perhaps not a good solution. We rarely get the chance to tell our side of the story after she has told hers. People don't tend to come to us looking to hear our truth. And so, the stark truth is that we can't prevent it. Part of the price of our freedom (whether that's total freedom, as in no contact, or emotional freedom, as in changing our behavior around her) is others' censure and judgment. No two ways about it.

Bluntly: You have to choose which price you'll pay—the price of being judged or the price of continuing to be abused. Your narcissistic mother has set it up so that one of those will apply, and most likely, you cannot overcome that. You get to choose. It's not a nice choice to have to make, and I take no joy in describing it so bluntly. But it is the reality.

As ever, there is no right or wrong about what you choose. Whatever works best for you in your specific circumstances is the right thing to do. Hopefully, seeing the options laid out like this will make the decision somewhat easier. That is my wish for you.

Don't forget that you can use EFT to help you decide, and also to cope with the sting of people's judgment.

Hugs,
Danu

WHO ARE YOU IN HER PRESENCE?

Dear DONM,

In this letter I want to talk about identity.

My mother often made it clear that she didn't like me. Of course she did, because it is part of the narrative of the narcissist that everything is the other person's fault. She often used to sigh to me, even when I was a child, "I love you, but I don't always like you." Thanks, Ma. (Actually, I never believed that she loved me either. I somehow always knew, deep down, that she didn't. As we spoke of already, when someone says they love you, it should feel like they do, and it never, ever felt like that.)

The thing is, I was a good child, as most DONMs are. We're always looking for their approval, and so we make damn sure to be good. Indeed, it was acknowledged in my home that I was the good one, but even so, any small thing seemed to provoke the "I don't like you" message.

But the thing is, in the later years of my relationship with her, I found that whenever I was in her company, I became someone I did not recognize and did not like. The stress of dealing with her and my father was so great that despite my best efforts, some of that stress leaked out, causing me to react snippily and sharply. I don't see how I could have done differently, however. I was in a total no-win situation. They (my father as well as my mother) were treating me as badly as they pleased, and any attempts of mine to discuss it with them ended up horribly.

So as long as I was in that toxic situation, my only options were to endure, and, being human, my endurance was not 100 percent successful, so the anger and hurt and exasperation and pain leaked out more than I would have liked. No matter that I swallowed 95 percent of the hurt and comebacks and challenges and arguments that she provoked; the other 5 percent leaked out despite myself. I became snippy and sharp sometimes, which is not like me. And I became closed down, and my normal animated self would disappear to be replaced by a stony-faced person.

This was perhaps the most subtle and yet most damaging aspect of the toxic relationship: not so much who she was to me (which was bad enough, of course), but who she made me be to myself. I did not like the person I was in her company. The toxicity and stress of the relationship caused me to react in ways that were not who I am. Not often, and not badly, but enough that it distressed me.

One of the many gifts of no contact is that I do not have to experience that shut-down and snippy and unhappy person anymore. I am free to be the person I really am.

I am sharing this in the hopes that it might resonate with you; that it might make you realize how you are in your mother's presence, as opposed to at other times; that you might realize that that person is not you, just the mask you have to wear to be able to survive the toxicity; and that you are able to compare and contrast and realize just how you are different in her presence (if indeed you are), and know who you really are.

Hugs,
Danu

WHY WE NEED TO BELIEVE THAT OUR PARENTS ARE ESSENTIALLY GOOD

Dear DONM,

I know from my reading on child psychology that children need to believe that their parents are good. This is because parents (or other caregivers) are essential to a child's survival. The child needs to believe that the parents are good enough to ensure their survival. If the child were to allow herself to realize that some parents are not good, it would be too terrifying, as then she would have to accept that her own survival could be in doubt.

Of course, if the parents are bad, the child's survival is at risk anyway, but it's too traumatic for the child to even consider that. So a child blames herself, rather than her parents, for their cruelties.

Another reason for this belief is because if the child's suffering is her own fault, then she can do something to fix it. She has (in her mind) the power to change the bad situation. If it's the parents' fault, then the child is truly powerless, and that's too traumatic to even begin to accept.

This is partly why we DONMs have such difficulty even seeing the abuse that was done to us. We are in denial. The other reason is gaslighting, of course. We are told early and often that it's all our fault, and of course we believe it, children being disposed to believing their parents. This, too, is a survival mechanism as, with good parents, it makes sense to believe them and trust in their greater wisdom.

With our mother/parents lying to us, and our own nature lying to us, it's no wonder we struggle so hard to see the truth. In my experience, the most common time women realize it is when they're in their forties. It takes four decades of abuse before we can realize it.

For sure, it's a liberation when we realize the truth. But it's traumatic too, of course. It's a huge step to acknowledge that, despite our strong wish and fervent belief, our parents were not good.

This, too, is why it's so hard to share this information with siblings. They have their own investment in their belief about our parents' goodness and may not be ready to hear anything different.

It all makes sense when you see it from this perspective. It's good to be gentle with ourselves, and with others, when we or they are slow to be able to allow the truth.

Hugs,
Danu

OTHERS' REACTIONS WHEN YOU TRY TO TELL THEM ABOUT NARCISSISTIC PERSONALITY DISORDER

Dear DONM,

We've spoken about how children need to believe that their parents are good. I suspect that this works on a societal level as well as an individual level. In other words, we as a society apply this need to believe in parents' goodness not only to our own parents but to parents in general.

A world in which parents are bad and cruel and abusive is not a world we feel safe living in. It's true that people know there are bad parents out there; the news leaves us in no doubt about that. But somehow we manage to see those as the odd exceptions, and all other parents as good. Our need to believe is so strong that we are willing to lie to ourselves.

As I said before, I have read that the reason we have fairy tales about wicked stepmothers rather than wicked mothers is so we can speak of the horrible things mothers can do while retaining the myth of the perfect mother. That makes sense to me.

The result of this is that our friends may struggle to believe us when we speak of our narcissistic mother's cruelties. The subtle cruelties are easily deniable. And it doesn't help that often it is so insidious that it's hard for us to even explain.

If we say, "She said it was great I'd lost weight, but she had that look in her eye that meant she was really furious," they're likely to say we imagined the look. What mother wouldn't be delighted with her daughter looking good? If we say, "She said I'd lost weight, but that was her way of reminding me how much weight I've put on," they'd think we were looking for an insult where one didn't exist.

If we try to share the more overt cruelties, they just don't believe it. They simply cannot conceive of a mother being so proactively cruel. So if we say, "She ironed a hole in my prom dress an hour before I was due to go out in it," they insist it must have been an accident. If we say, "She poisoned my dog because she couldn't bear that I got love and joy and comfort from him," they'll wonder about our sanity, and will explain that dogs get ill and die by themselves.

Even well-meaning friends can invalidate us. Not cruelly or abusively as our mother does, but for the above reasons. The result is the same though: we are invalidated, and that is hard when probably the very thing we are looking for most is validation.

I'm torn as to what is the best thing to do in this case. I think the ideal is that we do not seek validation from our friends. It's difficult in most cases for them to give because of this societal belief, and in a way it's not their job either.

But having said that, I do think it's very worthwhile to speak the truth about narcissistic personality disorder. Most people don't know it exists, or if they have heard of it, they vaguely think it's got something to do with vanity. The more there are people who know about NPD, the harder it will be for narcissists to get away with it. As it is, they hide in plain sight because so few people know about them.

So the trick, maybe, is to inform rather than to look for validation. To share the information calmly, without expecting any specific response. Easier said than done, I know—I am just exploring all this myself, and I don't pretend to have absolute answers. But hopefully you will have gotten some perspective out of my thoughts.

Hugs,
Danu

NARCISSISTS HIDE IN PLAIN SIGHT

Dear DONM,

As I mentioned in the last letter, narcissists get away with so much because so few people know about narcissistic personality disorder. They get away with their lies and manipulations and tantrums and ego trips and abuse.

Now that I know about NPD, whenever I meet anyone new, especially anyone who might want to be part of my life, I assess carefully whether they are narcissistic or not. There have been a few cases in which I have clearly realized someone is narcissistic, and I remove myself quietly from their company.

But others, those who don't know about NPD, cannot do that, and it leaves them vulnerable and open to the narcissistic abuse. Narcissists are very good at what they do—seducing their victims (either literally in the case of lovers, or metaphorically) to get them hooked and under their control so the fun and games of the abuse can begin.

Or, in the case of mothers and fathers, they don't do the seduction thing because they start ahead of the game—with their victim in their clutches. As we have discussed, people find it hard to believe that mothers can be cruel, because they're predisposed to believing mothers are good. But also, it doesn't help that if they don't know about NPD, they don't understand why someone would be cruel and nasty in those petty and immature ways.

It makes perfect sense once you understand NPD, but until then it seems unbelievable. The thinking seems to be like this: Why would someone go to the trouble of deliberately ruining your prom dress (to use my previous example)? What's in it for them? Why would they make you miserable at no gain to themselves?

It doesn't make sense until you know about NPD. So let's tell them about it.

But people, I find, don't want to know about NPD. They don't want to know that such senselessly nasty people are among us. That is changing somewhat as NPD has moved a little bit more into the public consciousness, but still, my overall sense is that most people don't know about it.

Those of us who talk about narcissistic personality disorder can be like the heroes in 1950s B-movies. There are aliens among us, pretending to be human, passing so well that they fool almost everyone. But those few of us who know the truth try to tell the others, and they just don't get it. They think we're crazy, or making it up, or taking things out of context, or . . . or . . . or . . . whatever it takes for them to keep their illusion that there are no aliens, that everyone is a nice, cooperative, empathetic human.

I can understand this. Knowing about narcissism is horrible; it's a murky and difficult situation. Far nicer to refuse to see it. But refusing to see it doesn't make it go away. We still have to live with it. And that refusal to see lets narcissists get away with so much: they hide in plain sight, and most people refuse to see.

In that case, those of us who know can, in small steps, educate the world—if we feel up for that (our own safety and healing must come first). In small ways, then, this is how we reclaim our power over these narcissists: by slowly cutting off their hiding place.

Hugs,
Danu

PRACTICING SAYING NO

Dear DONM,

We spoke before about being healthily selfish. As a follow-up to that, here's a suggestion for you to take, or not, as you find useful (as indeed, all my suggestions are). I wonder if it would be worth your while to practice saying no. Just to get used to it—to the feeling of it, and the process, and the reactions you get.

Not an abrupt or a rude "no," but a graceful, yet emphatic, one. You don't have to give reasons either. One of my favorite quotes is from Phoebe in the sitcom *Friends*: "Oh, I wish I could help, but I don't want to."

Okay, that was for comedic value and I don't suggest you use quite those words, but like a lot of comedy, it speaks truth through exaggeration, and the basic point is worthwhile: We don't have to make excuses. We don't have to get their agreement or permission to decline the request by coming up with a compelling enough excuse.

One phrase I find helpful is "Unfortunately, I'm not in a position to do that." Or, a little more softly, "I'm sorry, but I'm not in a position to do that." It's a reason without a reason, in a way. It sounds like you're explaining why you can't, so that you are not offering a blunt, abrupt "no"; however, in reality you're offering no information at all and you're not making any excuses.

One reason it's good to not explain yourself is simply that you don't owe anyone an explanation. Not wanting to is reason enough. (Obviously, if you can't drive an injured friend to the hospital, say, I think it's fair to say they'd deserve a genuine explanation. But most of the things you will be asked to do don't fall into that category.)

The other advantage to not giving a reason is that reasons can be overcome. If you say, "I'm sorry I can't do that as I have to pick Laura up from school," they can insist you'll be finished with their request before it's time to get Laura.

It might not sit well with you to do this, as you are most likely trained by your narcissistic mother to never put your own wants or needs first, or even to have put them on the list at all. It might be your default to agree to others' expectations, to almost get their permission before turning down their request. This concept might be very challenging for you. Obviously, I don't want you to do anything that's wrong for you, but I do invite you to consider that sometimes it's good to move beyond what is comfortable. What is comfortable isn't always right; sometimes it's just the bad situation we're used to. If you agree with this, you could practice playing with the concept of saying no without explanation.

Of course, I'm not recommending you turn into a begrudging, selfish woman who never helps anyone, but rather that you seek to flex the "no" muscle, to practice using it so you are comfortable with it when you need to. This is about redressing the balance and making sure your "yes" comes from a place of strength and willingness, not a place of default and obligation.

Another option is to make it a default to say, "I don't know yet if I'm able to do that; let me get back to you by [some reasonable time in the future]." That way, you're not caught off guard saying yes as a default.

It's still good to practice saying no, though! Once you get used to it, the benefits are really good. You feel (or at least, I did) stronger and much more empowered. When you agree to do things, you do them with a full heart and don't feel begrudging or manipulated into them. You have more time as you are no longer saying yes to everything, and you are better able to prioritize what is important to you both for yourself and for your contribution to your community.

Hugs,
Danu

WHY NARCISSISTS ARE NEVER WRONG

Dear DONM,

I was thinking recently of tells.

A tell is a phrase from poker, where bluffing is so important, and players can have a little tic or habit that gives away when they are bluffing. Tapping their forefinger on the table, maybe.

A huge narcissistic tell is that she never admits to making a mistake. Not truly. There might be a faux-admission in there, something along the lines of "I'm sorry you thought I didn't do it right" or "I'm sorry I didn't do it to your satisfaction" (the implication being that your standards are unreasonably high rather than that her achievement is unreasonably low, of course). Or maybe they'll abuse the passive voice: "Mistakes were made." But I think even such false admissions are rare, and normally, you will find that they never, ever, ever, *ever* admit to doing anything wrong. So this tell, of never admitting any wrongdoing, is one way you know you're dealing with a narcissist.

It's also one of the many toxicities that makes dealing with a narcissist so difficult. Because, if they never do anything wrong or make a mistake, and something isn't perfect, well, then it has to be someone else's fault, right? That's only logical. And the someone else may well be you. This applies if the narcissist in question is your mother or your partner or a friend or a colleague. They'll spin and manipulate things so that it's you who's at fault.

I remember saying once to my own mother, back in the days when I was still trying to work things out with her, that she talks too much, ignoring me, and it's not a conversation at all. Her answer? "Well, you make me so nervous that I talk too much as a reaction." This is a small but accurate example of how they can spin everything. Others might be: "You made me do it"; "You provoked me"; "Well, if you hadn't left the glass on the draining board, I wouldn't have broken it."

What do you do about it? There's not a lot you can do. If it's a work situation, I think it's best to document absolutely everything. If you agree to something verbally, send them a quick email confirming your understanding of the conversation so they can't deny it later. If needed, you can use their own complaint about you (that you consistently mishear or misunderstand what they said) in order to have the reason for the email: "As I'm prone to misunderstanding, I'm sending you this to make sure I understood correctly. Please let me know if I got anything wrong, and if I don't hear from you, I'll take it that this is correct." In personal situations, as far as I can see, you're limited to our usual awful options: suck it up, or remove yourself and go no contact. By definition, they won't change or admit they're less than perfect, so . . .

There are no easy answers to all of this. But at least understanding their patterns arms us better.

Hugs,
Danu

WHAT NARCISSISTS WILL
NEVER EXPERIENCE

Dear DONM,

I have written before (in *You're Not Crazy*) of the joy of being wrong, and I'd like to explore that further here.

The one thing I keep thinking is this: I feel so sorry for narcissists. I hate them and despise them and fear them too. The pity doesn't negate that at all. But I know what they're missing out on, and I do feel sorry for them for that.

I know from my own experience that there is power and integrity in accepting responsibility when you mess up.

I know there is huge strength in knowing it's okay to mess up, that it's part of being human, and that it doesn't mean we are lesser people whenever we make mistakes.

I know that learning and growth and adventure happen on the edges of our lives rather than in the safe center, and the edge is where confusion and chaos and mistakes live too. I know that there is huge richness in being willing to live at least part of the time on those chaotic edges.

I know that the more comfortable I am with failure, not letting it define me or traumatize me, the more inevitable is my success as, without failure-induced trauma, it's easier for me to pick myself up and try again.

I know I don't have to live in constant terror of making a mistake and therefore having to acknowledge my own imperfection, because I have already acknowledged that imperfection and live in it daily. I live in the paradox of always striving to improve, but also being okay with who and where I am now. I don't always manage to live this paradox 100 percent, by the way; I mess that up too, by blaming myself for doing wrong at times, for example. But that's okay as well. I just strive to do better and improve on that too.

I know all these wonderful things, and I know too that narcissists will never know them. I know that they live in terror of anyone, even themselves, finding out they're less than perfect. Using my empathy (which they also don't have), I can somewhat imagine that terror, and even by my dim understanding of it, it seems like a pure hell.

And in those moments, I feel so sorry for these people with their narrow, terrified lives. I hate what they do, the chaos and misery they cause, the life sentences they create for their victims. But I can pity them too, and at times I do. That pity is powerful, because we cannot fear what we pity.

Hugs,
Danu

WHAT IF SHE REALLY DOES CHANGE?

Dear DONM,

One of the truisms we work with is that a narcissist will never change. But people sometimes write to me and ask, "Yes, but what if she does?"

Not often, but also not unheard of, a narcissistic mother will agree to change her behavior when she has been called on it. What then? It's very confusing for the daughters concerned. Should they take their mother at face value and work toward a relationship again, they ask? I think that by definition, if they're wondering this, their intuition knows it's not right. But at the same time, they want to be fair. If their problem with their mother was x, or y, or z, and their mother has promised to no longer do x, or y, or z, surely they should give her another chance, shouldn't they? I think this one actually has an easy solution.

For a start, it's possible that their original guess was wrong, and that their mother does not have narcissistic personality disorder. Maybe she genuinely can change, and has changed. So there's an argument for taking her at face value and trying again. Here's the thing, though: a narcissist genuinely cannot change. If she is a narcissist, she will be guaranteed to give herself away, and before too long too.

Either she had no intention of changing, and just said it to draw her daughter back in, or she did want to change, as her desire for her daughter's company was, in the moment when she said it, stronger than her need to do the x, y, or z behavior. In the first instance, she won't make any practical attempts to change and will give herself away immediately. But even in the second case, it won't last. The effort of keeping that change against her nature will be too much for her, and she will soon revert to her usual patterns.

Have you ever tried to hold the same poles of magnets together? North-to-north or south-to-south? Picture the effort required to do that, and the fact that as soon as you stop applying the effort, they swivel in the ways they need to go. That's what it's like for a narcissist trying to change. It won't last.

So, I think there is no risk in allowing her to prove herself. You will soon know the truth for sure.

Hugs,
Danu

NARCISSISTS AS VICTIMS

Dear DONM,

The interesting thing is that if narcissists are called on their behavior, they can turn quickly to playing the victim. It's so backward—they can do or say whatever they like to you, but if you call them on it, no matter how mildly or calmly, they react as if you assaulted them.

They might go directly to victimization, or they might go via the paths of denial (gaslighting), anger/bullying, and then on to victimization. The gaslighting will take all the forms we've discussed before, and you can read about them in more detail on my website: "I did not say that!" or "Oh, you take everything too seriously."

If you insist on your point—"Even so, I would prefer if you didn't mention my weight in front of other people, as it really hurts me and upsets me"—she will immediately respond with anger and bullying. This is designed to put you back in your place: "How dare you speak to me like that! I'm your mother!" or "Well, you think you're so perfect, missy, let's talk about *your* faults for a change." And if you, heart quaking, continue (as I have done in my time), "Still, I would prefer if you didn't mention my weight in front of other people," the victim act will start.

This victimization, whether they leap to it first or come to it via the scenic route, will be extreme and, frankly, will seem like overkill. All you said was, "Mom, I really would prefer it if you didn't mention my weight in front of other people, as it hurts and upsets me when you do," and here you are being faced with full-blown crying, tears streaming down her cheeks as she sobs, "I don't know why you're so mean to me. I can't say anything around you! You take everything I say wrong. I was only trying to help, and this is the thanks I get. I can't do anything right for you!"

For sure, the details might not be exact, but the script won't vary by much. Additionally, it seems that the worse you're upset, the worse their reaction. Surely, you might think, they would want to comfort you if you're upset, not react so badly? Well, no, because . . . narcissists.

What is going on in their head when all this happens? I don't know, of course. My best guess, though, after years of trying to figure it out when my mother did this and reading up on it, is this: When you show negative reaction to her behavior, she genuinely does feel attacked. It makes sense when you think about it: She believes, and the survival of her whole psyche depends on her continuing to believe, that she's perfect. And here you are, pointing out to her that she's not perfect! Of course it's an attack (in her experience).

The worse your pain, the deeper the implied criticism of her perfection. If you're mildly upset by what she did, she's mildly imperfect, which is bad enough. But if you're deeply wounded, then she's deeply imperfect, and so she cannot possibly allow that reality to exist. She has to turn it back to you, to deflect it away from herself.

It does make perfect logical sense, no matter how hard it is to deal with. And of course it means that the whole topic is deflected because suddenly you're the bad guy. How did that happen? You end up apologizing to her or comforting her. Your own legitimate issue never gets mentioned again, let alone resolved. It makes perfect sense for them to react this way because their feelings are genuine, but also because it serves a very good purpose for them, making sure they're never accountable for their actions.

Hugs,
Danu

WHY CAN'T YOU TAKE CRITICISM?

Dear DONM,

One thing about these clever, manipulative narcissists is that they are able to subvert normal things for their benefit. We've spoken about this before, in how they get to create no-win situations. Here is another way they do this: they take something that is a normal part of human interactions, such as criticism, and they abuse that too. Their line for this dynamic is: "You can't take criticism."

That sounds like a valid thing to say. Because it's good to be able to take criticism, isn't it? None of us should think we're above that. (I'm sure you're spotting the irony already. I will come back to this below.) And so she gets to criticize you, and you have to take it. You don't understand why it feels so horrible and soul-destroying. Maybe you say to yourself, "Well, of course it's going to feel bad; criticism is never fun." The trap, of course, is that this is not criticism. It is verbal and emotional abuse masquerading as authentic criticism.

I have been thinking about the difference between authentic criticism and this abuse, and here are my thoughts on this:

Authentic criticism is about what you are doing—that is, your actions. It is no reflection on who you are as a person. On the contrary, in a healthy relationship it is a measure of their regard for you as a person that they want the relationship to be better, rather than ending it.

Verbal abuse masquerading as honest criticism tells you what the speaker thinks is wrong with who you are, rather than what's wrong with what you are doing.

Authentic criticism is designed to get you to change your behavior in order to function better in your relationship with the criticizer. It's saying, in effect, "Here is a problem, and you need to solve it." It will have the solution inherent in the criticism: "I don't like the way you do x. Could you do y instead?" Or the solution might be clear from the criticism: if someone complains about you leaving the cap off the toothpaste, then the solution is clearly to put the cap back on in the future.

Toxic criticism has no such solution. It doesn't want to solve the problem. It's not aimed at making you improve. Indeed, they don't really want to change the situation, as then they'd have no stick to beat you with. Verbal abusers want to keep you squashed and fearful and in the wrong. Toxic criticism is designed to break you and intimidate you and keep you docile.

Because it doesn't want solutions, toxic criticism will be so vague and broad as to be meaningless. The criticism might be: "You are so oversensitive." Note the words "You are"—this is making an absolute statement about you as a person. Note, too, that the complaint is so vague and all-encompassing that it's impossible to know how to fix it. How does this oversensitivity manifest?

Say you really are oversensitive. I think a lot of DONMs can genuinely become a little bit oversensitive. I know I can lean that way myself, and it's something I have to constantly watch. It's not surprising, when we were living on edge all the time, when we were criticized constantly for who we were, etc. So for argument's sake, let's say that's true and a valid criticism.

In that case, authentic criticism would be something like: "When I occasionally can't meet you, please don't get so upset." Do you see how that's specific and solvable? You can, if you agree there's merit in the criticism, look at your behavior and come up with some way of handling it better. But "You're so oversensitive" leaves you nowhere to go. How do you begin to solve that?

Now, it's possible that even a well-meaning person might not have the skills to articulate what's going on and will resort to a blanket statement such as "You're too oversensitive." In this case, though, you could tease it out with them: "In what ways am I oversensitive? Can you help me understand?" A genuine person will respond to that, and you both could have a constructive conversation about it until you get to the root of what's bothering them and work on a solution that meets both your needs.

I suspect that if you tried that with a narcissistic mother, it wouldn't go so well. She doesn't want to solve the problem, after all; she wants her metaphorical stick to beat you with. So, if you asked her to help you understand, I bet you'd get something like "Oh, for heaven's sake! I'm not going to be able to give you every example! You're doing it all the time, and we'd be here all day if I were to start."

So that is one way to tell the difference: Is it about problem-solving, or about criticism for its own sake? Or if the toxic criticism, by some chance, was specific enough for you to address it, you'd find that doesn't work either. They'll either find something else to criticize you about or will change their mind about what they want. So, for example, if they criticize you for always putting the new toilet paper on the roll the wrong way, and you change how you do it to how they said, then that will become the wrong way, and when you say, "But that's what you wanted," they'll gaslight you and insist it wasn't.

Even if toxic criticism is specific, it also extrapolates to being about you as a horrible person. For example:

Authentic criticism: "I really would prefer it if you put the cap back on the toothpaste."

Authentic frustrated criticism: "I hate it when you leave the cap off the toothpaste. I've told you over and over. Please, please, stop doing that!"

Toxic criticism: "I hate it when you leave the cap off the tooth-paste. I've told you over and over. You're so careless. You don't care about my needs at all. You're an absolute loser. You've been a trial to me since the day you were born. I wish I had aborted you."

Authentic criticism is also about something that's reasonable to ask, whereas toxic criticism will most likely be unreasonable. Okay, defining what's reasonable is a whole other conversation. Is it reasonable to put the toilet seat down or leave it up? That one won't be resolved anytime soon! But although there are blurry parts in the middle, most times the distinction will be clear. It's reasonable to ask someone to text or phone if they're going to be late. It's not reasonable to expect someone to mind-read what you want for your birthday and to criticize them if they got the wrong thing when you refused to tell them what you wanted.

I encourage you to assess what criticism you receive to see if it is authentic criticism or toxic criticism. It's good to listen to authentic criticism and evaluate it to see if it's fair. Toxic criticism is not about you or your behavior, but about abuse, and so is a very different thing.

Of course, the irony mentioned above is that your narcissistic mother, who thinks it's terrible that you can't take criticism, is a person who can never, ever take even the gentlest or most reasonable criticism herself. I'm sure you've experienced how any mild criticism of her is greeted with fury and denial and tears and absolute rejection of whatever you're saying. And woe to the DONM who says to her narcissistic mother, "You can't take criticism." Don't try that at home, folks.

Hugs,
Danu

WHAT ABOUT WHEN SHE'S OLD?

Dear DONM,

What do you do when your narcissistic mother gets old and needs care?

This is a really tough one, and I don't pretend to have the answers. I think there are no easy, one-size-fits-all answers. But hopefully I can tease through some thoughts that might help. Bear in mind that as ever, these are just my thoughts and not some expert view or sacred dogma. I will make my case and place my arguments, and if it makes sense to you, then that's great, but feel free to disagree with every word. Still, even if you do disagree with every word and think my arguments don't have any validity, I hope that disagreement will help you to clarify your own thoughts on the matter.

Also bear in mind that as I discuss this, it is all hypothetical for me. I have not actually been faced with this dilemma.

I have, however, thought long and hard about it because I wanted to be prepared for it if that moment did come. And I share these thoughts here.

I realize that it is very much part of the social contract that adult children look after their elderly parents, and it has been that way since forever, in all cultures. It is a bit blurred these days with pension plans and care centers and so on. But for most of human history we didn't have those, so the deal was that the parent looked after the child when they were young, and the child returned the favor in due course when the parent became old and helpless in their turn.

My view, however, is that our narcissistic mothers have already broken that deal. She didn't fulfill her half of the bargain. Oh, okay, she did, to an extent. If you're reading this, you're still here, and so she raised you well enough so that you survived into adulthood. She didn't kill you either through neglect or intention. But that's setting the bar very low, isn't it?

I know it sounds like a petulant teenager to say this, but: we didn't ask to be born. I don't think my son owes me anything for the care and love I poured into his upbringing. To me, it was my decision to have a baby, and therefore it was my responsibility and obligation to provide for him, both materially and emotionally. It wasn't a favor I was doing him. So when I say that it was my mother's decision to have the baby that was me, and therefore it was her responsibility and obligation to care for me, I am being consistent. And truly, she fulfilled her responsibility very poorly, as did your mother.

I don't feel I owe her a damn thing, frankly. I wouldn't anyway, just as my son doesn't owe me anything, but if she had been a better mother and a nicer person and had treated me well enough, I may well have wanted to care for her out of love and gratitude. But that situation doesn't apply.

So with the situation as it is, I truly don't think I owe her any care in her old age. I don't wish her ill. I would not be proactively nasty to her. I don't make this decision in a sense of revenge or bitterness. It's just that she is a stranger to me, and I am not responsible for strangers' well-being.

Will others judge me for taking that stance? For sure. The belief that we should look after our elderly parents is deep in our culture, and I am rejecting that. Of course, people will have opinions. And it is part of being human that we want others' opinions of us to be good. Many emails I get deal with this issue—how neighbors and others will judge the writer if she doesn't look after her mother or parents—and I understand how that social disapproval looms large.

It's up to each of us how we handle that dilemma, because I do not think we can avoid it. For me, the price of others' negative opinion is a lower price than the price of years of my life and the bruising to my self that caring for my mother would cost me. It seems unfair that I have to pay any price, but that is the reality, and so I get to choose which price I pay. (As do you.)

I won't live my life in a way that's toxic to me just to satisfy others' opinions of how things should be done. And those same others, don't forget, don't know the whole story or even part of it. The abuse I experienced is hidden abuse, and they do not see it. I would love to explain it to them and therefore get their understanding of my decision and maybe even their approval of it. But that's not possible.

And so, I make my choice that I do not owe my parents care in their older years and that I will not be there for them. Quite apart from everything else, I'm still spending too much time and energy trying to belatedly build my own life, to repair the damage they have created, to have time and energy for that.

As for what you decide—I do not pretend to know what's right for you. But hopefully this will have helped clarify your thinking one way or another.

Hugs,
Danu

WHAT ABOUT FEELING COMPASSION FOR HER?

Dear DONM,

If you do end up looking after her, though, you might struggle with being unable to feel kindness for her. Quite a few DONMs have written to me to ask how to feel compassion for their mother.

Here is what I think about that (and as ever, judge what I say on its own merits, and see if it makes sense to you):

My first thought is always about how wonderful these women are, to even seek to feel compassion for their abusers. I think how their narcissistic mothers had absolute jewels of daughters and didn't even realize it. Their daughters were diamonds, and all they did was heap dirt on top of those diamonds. But the diamonds remain intact under the dirt, and the narcissistic mother will never know it, in her self-absorption. That is her (the narcissistic mother's) loss, no matter that she'll never even know there was something like that to lose. (It's the daughter's loss too, to never be appreciated for the diamond she is, of course.)

So this bruised and abused daughter is still seeking to find compassion for her mother, and I am in awe of that.

About compassion itself, and seeking to feel it and feeling bad if you can't:

My thoughts are that we can feel a kind of distant compassion, compassion for her physical frailties and the other limitations of age, just as we would for any stranger, but that we are not obliged in any way to feel deep and loving compassion for her.

That kind of thing is the product of a lifetime's healthy relationship, and our mothers did not allow that plant to flourish at all. Our lack of compassion is simply the consequence of her behavior.

I don't know how you can capture full compassion for her. I am not even sure that you need to try. If you are doing the actions of caring for her, that is a huge and wonderful thing to do for someone who has abused you. I'm not sure you need to beat yourself up over having all the "wrong" feelings on top of that. The actions are the thing.

It is, of course, essential to be kind to her and not abuse her in turn, but I'm not sure she is entitled to anything more than a distant professional kindness such as a nurse would offer. And she is lucky to get that, frankly.

Hugs,
Danu

WHAT DOES JAPANESE POTTERY HAVE TO DO WITH BEING A DONM?

Dear DONM,

I recently came across the Japanese concept of *kintsugi*. What this means is, when a pottery bowl breaks, they glue it back together with gold lacquer. If you do an online search for "kintsugi," you will see beautiful examples.

In this way the cracks are not hidden as if they're something shameful, but rather are celebrated. It's as if they are saying: "This bowl has had a life, and things happened in that life, and we now see the story of those events, and that is fine."

I think we DONMs can be like this, if we choose. We have been left with dreadful scars by our upbringing. But we can accept and celebrate those scars as part of who we are, rather than being ashamed of them. They are part of our lived experience.

In kintsugi, artisans fit the bowl smoothly back together. They don't leave it shattered on the ground. It needs to be fit for purpose. In the same way, we do our best to shape our lives into a smooth and cohesive whole. We pick up the pieces off the floor and shape them into the best life we can. This isn't about living with the breakage. It's about mending our lives in a proud and assertive way, rather than a furtive and ashamed way.

Yes, our lives are pieced together rather than always having been whole, but the fixing together is part of us, and is to be acknowledged and even valued as such.

Hugs,
Danu

"STOP THE SILLINESS"

Dear DONM,

One thing I've seen again and again with narcissistic mothers is that if their daughter pulls away or stops contacting them or whatever, there can be various strategies. One of them is silence as the narcissistic mother waits to see who'll crack first. And it's often the daughter, as she cannot bear the silence, so the intimidation works.

Another strategy is tears and sobs of "I don't know what I've done to deserve this." Another is playing the victim: "She's being mean to me."

But one that comes up again and again is a kind of finger-snapping: "This nonsense has gone on long enough!" or "Stop this silliness, *now!*" It might be your narcissistic mother saying this, or one of her flying monkeys. But the effect is the same, regardless of who the mouthpiece is.

I have to say, I struggle to think of a more arrogant, dismissive reaction. To them, whatever is going on to cause you to behave like this, it is not to be taken seriously. Nor is it important to discuss things with you, to ask what's wrong, and to try to fix it somehow. Oooooh, no. Nope. It is to be dismissed as mere childish sulking. This totally undermines you, invalidates you, and dismisses you. It is also a clear refusal to deal with the issue, and a demand that you return to the way things were before.

It's not surprising, of course, that she wants things to return like that. The way things were before was working for her. It's how she had it set up, to suit herself. Of course she wants it that way, and is eager for it to return to that way as soon as possible. Equally naturally, that arrogant, authoritarian way of speaking is very intimidating to us. It was the way we were raised; we are trained to respond to it, and we often still do. We start believing how she has framed it: that we are being nonsensical or silly or absurd or unreasonable or however she phrases it.

And so, it's quite likely we'll fall for it and, indeed, stop the silliness. Except, of course, it's not silliness, is it? It's not nonsense. It's what we have been driven to by years of her behavior and her inability to listen to us or to treat us right. Her response to our reaction to her abuse is just more of the abuse—being dismissive and invalidating, and resolving nothing.

It seems to me it would be good to be aware of how manipulative and inappropriate it is to call someone's reaction silliness or nonsense, and to know we don't have to fall for it.

Hugs,
Danu

SOME THOUGHTS ON RESOLVING
RELATIONSHIP ISSUES

Dear DONM,

Another thought that occurs to me is that in unhealthy relationships nothing is ever resolved. There may be fights—there certainly were between me and my parents whenever I'd try to discuss anything with them, no matter how calmly I'd start.

I'd withdraw, shaking, and then time would pass, and next time we'd meet, it would be business as usual, no mention of what happened before, and no resolution to it. And this pattern would repeat over and over. (Why, yes, I am a slow learner. Why do you ask?)

I think I've realized now that in a healthy relationship, there are three partners, in a way. There is you, and me, and the relationship as an entity that we both value. If there's a problem, it's a problem within the relationship that needs to be resolved, and so both of us will work to do that very thing. It's not about blame as such, or one of us needing to be wrong, but of something not working right. So we approach it in a spirit of problem-solving.

In a toxic or abusive relationship, the only thing that matters is "me," and any complaints are to be quashed immediately so I can carry on as I always have.

In a healthy relationship, each person's issues will be taken seriously. They might not automatically be agreed with, but they'll be acknowledged and discussed, not dismissed out of hand.

It has become something essential for me in a relationship that if I say, "I don't like when you do x," they take it seriously and calmly. My job, of course, is to say it calmly and not nastily or aggressively, approaching it as a problem to be solved rather than as a personal fault. I go into that discussion knowing I might be wrong or unreasonable or have too high expectations. I don't for one minute think I'm always right. But I try to think my issue through myself first, to see if I am reasonable to expect this (whatever the "this" might be) and to resolve it myself, if I'm not reasonable, by changing my own expectations.

But I am aware that even with my best intentions, I might be wrong, so I am fully open to discussing it and changing my expectations if that's appropriate.

Likewise, if someone comes to me with an issue, I do my best to accept it calmly, knowing that to do so is not to automatically assume I am wrong or at fault, but that something isn't working in a relationship I value, so it needs to be fixed one way or another. This isn't easy. My default reaction is to be defensive and resistant. But as part of trying to be a healthy, functioning person in a healthy, functioning relationship, I acknowledge that part of me and reassure myself that it's okay, and then I try to be present in the discussion.

There is, ideally and usually, no fight, but there is a resolution, and we form our relationship rules a bit better, and so it works better going forward.

This is so different from how narcissists do it. They don't want to resolve anything, as we well know. But we are looking for healthier models than that, of course, and this is one that works for me, so I'm sharing it with you to see if you will find it useful too.

Hugs,
Danu

THE TWO-SIDES FALLACY

Dear DONM,

You'll often hear it said that there are two sides to every story, or as a variation, that there are three sides to a story: yours, theirs, and the truth. People often use this saying to minimize or invalidate what you are going through with your narcissistic mother.

They might be genuine people who truly believe this and are trying to help you as best they can by saying that she's not so bad really, or maybe she didn't mean to hurt your feelings, or whatever. Or they might be your narcissistic mother's flying monkeys who just want to stop you from rocking the boat. But in either case, of course, they are wrong. There sometimes is absolutely only one side to the story. Sometimes your side is the real truth.

I know that when humans interact, there are nuances and misunderstandings and failed assumptions and all sorts of things that make our communications complex and clumsy and open to failure. So yes, often there are two sides to the story, for sure. Just not when it's a case of absolute abuse, including narcissistic abuse.

But I think people don't like thinking of abuse. They'd rather think people are well-meaning and it's all a misunderstanding. They don't want their worldview rocked by having to know the truth about the abuser. This is why people sometimes even—hideously—do the two-sides thing about sexual abuse: "What did you do to entice him?" or "Could you not have said no?"

I think, too, that DONMs often go too far in the way of seeing the other person's point of view. We've been taught that all our lives, after all. So when someone says to us, "Well, there are two sides to a story," we can find ourselves thinking of our own faults and how we contributed to the problem.

And truthfully, as humans, we're not perfect, and I'm not saying that we are. But honestly, I think that with narcissists it's pretty much guaranteed that the fault is 100 percent theirs, or nearly so anyway. Especially since they have us so well trained and scared that we make sure to be nice to them, give in to them, and so on.

I think we need to keep this in mind when dealing with them, and not fall for the two-sides fallacy. For sure, we should keep an eye on our own behavior, as we don't want to fall into the narcissistic never-at-fault fallacy. (Not that I think there'll be much worry about that.) But know that if she's narcissistic, she's almost guaranteed to be the one in the wrong, no matter how much she insists she's 100 percent in the right. So judge accordingly.

You probably can't stop the two-sides apologists from doing their thing. Flying monkeys are motivated to keep to the party line, and the genuine people really do believe it.

But make sure you know the truth and don't fall into the trap of thinking it's equally your fault.

Hugs,
Danu

"BUT SHE WANTS ME BACK! DOESN'T THAT MEAN SHE LOVES ME?"

Dear DONM,

DONMs often write to ask me this: "If my mother hates me so much and is so aware of all my flaws, as she keeps sharing them with me, why is she so upset now that I'm not seeing her?"

Why, they wonder, is the narcissistic mother sending flying monkeys and/or contacting her incessantly (to the point of stalking sometimes)? Her pleas and entreaties sound so genuine. It really sounds as if the narcissistic mother sincerely misses her daughter.

Surely, the narcissistic mother should be glad to be free of such a horrible daughter. But if so, why is she so devastated? It doesn't make sense, does it? The poor DONM's thoughts go round and round like a hamster wheel, trying to reconcile this apparent contradiction.

Often—totally understandably—they start to wonder if they misjudged their mother. Maybe she does really love them after all, and that's why she can't let them go. Along with this dilemma there's a huge dose of guilt for making their narcissistic mother suffer so much. The daughter hears from the flying monkeys just how upset her mother is, crying and weeping and sobbing. No wonder the DONM feels guilty. Maybe, she thinks, she should go back to her mother and try again and see if the relationship could work this time. And yet, and yet . . . and round and round the thoughts go.

This seeming dilemma makes sense, though, when you realize what's really going on for the narcissistic mother. Yes, she genuinely does miss her daughter. But think of it this way: Have you ever seen a cat that brought a dead mouse home and had it taken away? Remember how the cat is so upset and sad and meows piteously at the loss and goes around the house trying to find it in corners?

The cat genuinely misses the mouse. But as its prey, its chew-toy. It does not want a healthy, loving, mutually respectful relationship with the mouse. And that, I would argue, is an exact analogy of how the narcissistic mother feels. The narcissist's addiction, don't forget, is to the drug of attention: narcissistic supply, as it's called. If her daughter removes herself, then the mother has lost that source of narcissistic supply. No wonder she's devastated.

Add to this the fact that narcissists absolutely hate rejection. Okay, none of us likes rejection, but narcissists really, *really* hate it. They cannot bear it. You could almost say they are allergic to it. Again, this makes total sense because if they're so perfect, why would anyone reject them? And so, their daughter walking away is an implicit statement that they're not perfect, and of course, narcissists cannot bear that thought. They cannot bear rejection, and now their own daughter has rejected them. The sooner that situation is canceled out, the better.

Another factor might be that the narcissistic mother loves the drama. She can weep to all the potential flying monkeys about how devastated she is, how bereft, how sad. She can gather lots of attention and sympathy and "stroking" that way.

So those three factors—the chew-toy factor, the hate-rejection factor, and the love-drama factor—are all real and credible reasons the narcissistic mother will seek to get her daughter back. And none of those reasons involves loving her daughter, or respecting her daughter, or missing her daughter for who she actually is. None of those reasons involves any genuine wish or intention to improve the relationship.

If she's narcissistic, she does not love or respect or miss anyone. My point is that the narcissistic mother's distress is totally genuine, but it is not a sign that she loves her daughter. So, from the daughter's point of view, nothing has changed.

It can be very hard to really, *really* accept that she will never change and to let that hope go. But freedom—painful freedom, but freedom nonetheless—lies in accepting that.

I don't think there are any DONMs who have walked away from their mother on a whim or at the first sign of trouble. We all walked away after years and years and years of trying to work it out. Not only did the narcissistic mother not meet us halfway; she used our well-meaning efforts as a way to further abuse us. That's the reality. And all her tears and phone calls will not change that.

Hugs,
Danu

WHAT ABOUT DRAMA QUEENS?

Dear DONM,

Today I'm going to talk about drama queens. You know what I mean, I am sure.

Drama queens are the ones who love drama and crisis and upset, and who will provoke such things in their own lives because of the attention they can get for it.

They even love trauma and tragedy, or at least they love it when those are happening to other people and they get to witness it. They love to help, but this help is voyeuristic and self-indulging, giving them a ringside seat. (That is, if the help does actually offer the best views. If you ask for something unglamorous—"I'd love some help, thank you so much for offering. I wonder could you cook a few dinners for the freezer?"—you won't see her for dust.)

Drama queens are allergic to peace and quiet and tranquility, so if there isn't enough drama going on, they'll even create some. They'll decide they might have a terminal illness, or get a mystery allergy, or provoke a fight with a friend, or decide their husband's having an affair. Or something that to the rest of us would be just a blip in the day—temporarily losing our keys, for example—will become a crisis of the highest order for them. Anything to create drama. Drama queens can even sabotage themselves into losing a job, say, because something like that provides great drama.

People can be drama queens without being narcissists. (For example, it's a trait associated with NPD's "sister" disorder, histrionic personality disorder.) Conversely, perhaps not *all* narcissists are drama queens, but there's definitely a big overlap. Drama leads to attention, and as we know, narcissists need attention.

Drama queens are exhausting to be around. Most of us prefer to avoid drama, as it's stressful and overwhelming. Life brings enough crises all by itself without creating more. So being in the blast zone of all this drama is very challenging.

And yet, we might feel obliged to help the drama queen. That's what friends and family are for, right? If someone close to us loses her job or has a bad fight with her husband, shouldn't we be there for her? Help her, listen to her, support her?

It's a bit of a quandary, to be sure, especially since DONMs have been trained to be docile and pleasing. As a nice person, you want to be there for people when they need you. But if they need you too often, if they just seem so accident-prone and such a disaster-magnet, that might be a flag that they're a drama queen.

While we all want to vent, I think, whenever something major goes wrong, in most cases after a suitable vent, or after time to process what's happened, healthy people go about fixing the problem. They might still need your ear, but now they'll be saying things like, "Do you think solution A or solution B would be better?" The drama queen, on the other hand, will simply wallow in the issue, with no desire to fix it. Likewise, if you come up with suggestions, the healthy person will consider them genuinely. The drama queen will shoot down all practical suggestions immediately. She doesn't want solutions; she wants sympathy.

Be aware of the tone of it all. A healthy person is genuinely overwhelmed and upset about whatever crisis has happened. A drama queen is enjoying it; there'll be an air of excitement about her.

So how do you handle it? I tend, if possible, to ease away from drama queens altogether so I don't have to put up with them. I am aware that drama queens are manipulative and that they use people as drama fodder or audiences, so I feel no obligation to be with them.

If for any reason I'm stuck in their drama without escape, I make sure not to feed the drama in any way. I don't agree breathlessly with them that yes, it's terrible, and x is a horrible person and y shouldn't have happened and z is so unfair. I stay deliberately calm and deadpan, really: "I can see you're very upset about that, all right. But I have faith that you'll be able to overcome it." (I don't have that faith at all, of course, but it calls their bluff.)

Yes, I risk being accused of being very unsympathetic, but that's okay too. My real friends know I am sympathetic and supportive, and if a drama queen doesn't think so, well, she won't try to milk me for sympathy again, which is a win in my book.

Hugs,
Danu

WE ARE THE BONSAI CHILDREN

Dear DONM,

Those of us who were raised by narcissists are the "bonsai children."

The seed that was us was just as whole and full of glorious potential as every other seed. We had the wondrous, vibrant, audacious potential to grow deep roots to embrace the earth and spread exuberant branches to hug the sky. But we were not planted into freedom, into rich soil, with room for our roots to firmly claim our share of the earth and to anchor ourselves solidly, and from there to grow upward, strong and sturdy, reaching for the sky, branching out, green and vivid and hearty. No.

We were planted into a tiny pot. It might even have been a pretty pot, a ceramic pot with cute round feet and curlicues. It might have been an ugly pot, cracked and broken terracotta. But it was, for sure, a constraining, limiting, shackling pot. Our roots were hampered, growing only a minuscule distance before they reached the cold, hard, uncaring limits of the pot. They had no choice, these roots, but to remain tiny, puny things with only a tenuous hold on the little parcel of earth they had been allotted.

Some of us were watered well in that pot, and fed well. We were still stunted, though, by the inherent limits of the pot. Others of us were not even given enough of our basic needs; instead, we received inconsistent watering and very little food, so the stunting came from many angles.

With our roots so limited, and possibly our needs barely met, how could we grow tall and strong and solid?

We could not.

But just to be sure we did not grow to our potential, our young shoots were ruthlessly clipped and pruned to keep us small. Our tiny, hopeful branches were wrapped in tight coils of harsh, cold metal and then twisted and manipulated to make them grow in the shape desired by our creator—this desired shape being an imitation and a mockery of how we would look as adults, if left to grow freely. The desired shape of another, for whom our very existence, our very shape, our reality was a matter of their whim and preference over our own true needs.

From the thin, artificial soil of our pots we could see other trees. We saw how boldly and unapologetically they grew tall and strong. But even as we looked in awe and envy at the real trees, we did not realize that was our birthright too, stolen from us. We did not even realize we could aspire to grow as robustly. We thought that such strength and beauty was for other trees, better trees.

And so, we were small and weak and stunted and hobbled, and we blamed ourselves for it. A double pain: to be so less-than, and to be at fault for that. So many layers of shame.

Indeed, our creator blamed us too, if we dared to question it. *You'll never grow big and strong*, they'd sneer. *You're lucky we kept you at all. You're lucky we watered you when other trees access their own water. You're lucky we fed you when other trees work for their own nutrients. You are pathetic and you dare to question us who have given you everything?*

It seems true; it seems plausible. So our meager branches bow lower, and our tiny leaves quiver in the heat of the breath and spittle of their anger. This is what it means to be a bonsai child.

The biggest leap we'll ever take is the mental leap of knowing that the pot is not our true home, the metal binds not our true clothing.

After that, there's the physical leap to leave the pot and claim our birthright. But we carry the years of stunting with us, struggling to recover, to grow as strong and tall as the other trees do effortlessly. And maybe blaming ourselves for that struggle, not realizing that it's the grotesque legacy of being one of the bonsai children and none of our doing at all.

And we forget to applaud ourselves for having left the pot and for trying to grow beyond the pruning at all.

Until we remember.

Hugs,
Danu

THE QUEST FOR HER APPROVAL

Dear DONM,

   One thing that every DONM needs to realize for her own peace of mind is that she will never please her mother (or at least, not to a large extent and not for long—I speak more of this below). This is a hard and sad fact to accept, but peace and even a kind of freedom come from accepting it. You can let down the burden of trying to win her approval. Only then will you realize just how exhausting that burden was.

   So why can't you please her, no matter how hard you try? The fact is that she doesn't want to have you please her. That is too easy and too harmonious and too drama-free. She wants you on edge and anxious. She wants you vying for her approval. When you are hungry for that approval, you are focusing on her and giving her attention, and she's happy with that situation.

   The promise of her approval is the bait she wields to keep you trying. But like the carrot on the stick in that famous image of the donkey, the bait is always out of reach.

   Okay, she might well drop you a few crumbs of approval now and again, the amount being carefully judged to make you hopeful that her overall approval is an achievable goal. It's much like how casinos allow gamblers a carefully calculated number of wins, because if we always lost, we'd eventually give up. Of course, your mother doesn't want you giving up on your quest for her approval, so she will give small and temporary approval when needed.

My own mother used to say, her tone full of approval, "Oh, you're soooo good to do that!"—whatever "that" was. Bringing her food at the hospital every day because she didn't like the hospital food is one example I recall.

As I think of it, I see that the actions that gained her approval most were those that stroked her need for narcissistic supply. Bringing her food that I had cooked meant I was thinking of her while I cooked, and all the other patients in the ward got to see that she was getting special treatment. The time my sister and I spent hours cleaning her kitchen from top to bottom when she was out (she wouldn't have been a great housekeeper, to say the least) didn't garner nearly the same amount of approval. No, instead she was furious. Absolutely furious. She didn't say so, of course. She couldn't. She said thank you, briefly and begrudgingly, because she had to. But I could tell she was furious by her scowl and the fury emanating from her in almost-visible waves. It took me years to figure that one out, but of course it was because us cleaning the kitchen was, by definition, an implied (even though unintended) criticism of her housekeeping skills.

But she would approve whenever I did anything to stroke her narcissism. Whenever she said, "You're so good to do that," it used to stress me unbearably. This was long before I knew about narcissistic personality disorder, or even before I'd acknowledged that things weren't good, so I could never understand why I found it painfully difficult.

I think now it's that I realized that approval was so incredibly conditional. It was approval of that one action I had done, rather than any approval of who I am as a person. That approval was so temporary and fragile. That approval would be withdrawn fully and instantly the next time I didn't please her. And the disapproval was about who I am rather than about whatever "bad" thing I had done.

Being bad and disapproved of was my default state, it felt, and I was always trying to move away from that.

I now realize that was doomed to failure. Like that Greek fellow in the legend, Sisyphus, who was doomed forever to roll a stone up a hill, only to have it roll back down again to the bottom just before he reached his goal.

Our need for her approval is a powerful weapon she has over us, and it's one she brainwashed us with from our earliest days. However, this belief only has the power we give it. We can't help the fact that she brainwashed us with it, but we can reject the brainwashing now and choose to get our approval from ourselves instead of from her.

I am talking about approval of who we are as people, and that's our birthright. It doesn't mean we're perfect (because we're not). It means we're okay despite not being perfect. As one DONM wrote to me the other day: "We're imperfectly and wondrously made."

Sisyphus was stuck with his task, but the good news for us is that we can stop doing ours. We can just stop trying. Easier said than done, of course, but as ever, you can use EFT to help you. And as I said at the beginning of this letter, the freedom and release and peace you will feel are incredible.

Hugs,
Danu

WHAT DO TODDLERS AND NARCISSISTS HAVE IN COMMON?

Dear DONM,

I have realized one thing about narcissists: Whatever the question is, the answer is "toddler." I mean this as a metaphor, of course. But also, I think it's more than that—that narcissists are factually and genuinely still mentally and emotionally toddlers.

Toddlers think the world revolves around them. They struggle to see the difference between wants and needs. They have no sense of deferred gratification; when they want something, they want it now. They have no empathy; they cannot see how others might feel about things and, therefore, don't care about mistreating others. They will be sunny and cheerful when they get their way but turn to sobs and tantrums the minute they're thwarted. They have a rich fantasy life, being certain that if they think it's so, it must be so. And more, if they *say* it's so, it must be so.

Does any of this sound familiar? Can we replace the word *toddler* with *narcissist* and have it still make sense? I think so. Like toddlers, narcissists, particularly those on the milder end of the scale, can be genuinely fun and cheerful and pleasant to be around—right until they're not, of course. But once their narcissistic need for attention is met and their ego is being stroked, they can be rather lovely.

This is partly why we can have the confusing experience of thinking, as people often write to me, "But she can be so nice!" Of course she can. But the thing to remember is that it's only paper-thin niceness. It's a niceness caused by having everything her own way.

Both toddlers and narcissists have meltdowns when things don't go their way. We call it a tantrum when it's a toddler, and narcissistic rage when it's a narcissist. But they're pretty much the same thing.

The horrific thing is that these toddlers in adult bodies have power over their own children. Can you imagine a toddler being in charge of a household? What a terrifying scenario.

Of course, you don't have to imagine it. You lived it.

Hugs,
Danu

WHEN PEOPLE GUSH ABOUT HOW NICE SHE IS, WHAT DO YOU DO?

Dear DONM,

What do you say to people who aren't flying monkeys as such, but who wish to talk about your mother? Maybe people who are genuine, but who have her bending their ear about the fact that you aren't in touch, and who are therefore caught in the middle.

I think you would be justified in saying to them that this is nothing to do with your relationship with them and so you ask them not to speak to you about your mother. Furthermore, I would say that they are, in turn, entitled to say to your mother that they're not getting in the middle and do not wish to hear any more about you from her, as sometimes people genuinely don't realize they're allowed to not be part of a conversation they don't want to be part of.

But regardless of what they do, you don't want to hear any more about her, and your relationship with them has to be independent of that. (Of course, say it more softly and diplomatically than that, but that'd be the gist of it.)

And of course, when I say that you "ask" them to not speak to you about her, I am suggesting that that is the way you phrase it. In fact, you are *telling* them this and will enforce it via boundaries if needed. If they insist on talking to you about her, then they do fall into the category of flying monkeys and need to be dealt with accordingly.

If you meet casual acquaintances who know your mother and gush about her, then it's slightly different. Often narcissists can come across very well in a superficial way—they make it their business to do so, so they can get the approval and admiration they want. In superficial relationships they can hide their real selves, so people don't see through them.

So you might well have people gushing to you. They might say, "Oh, I loved your mother! She was such fun! So nice!" I've experienced this, and the temptation to tell the truth is very strong. But I just gritted my teeth and said lightly that I was glad they had such good memories of her; that she'd love to hear that. (That last bit was true, as she *would* love to hear it. But it wasn't a promise to tell her either!)

The real situation with my mother is not for sharing with casual acquaintances, so I will just thank them for their kind words and let it go, frustrating though that is.

Sometimes, though, you do want to try to explain, and we talk about this next.

Hugs,
Danu

SO HOW *DO* YOU EXPLAIN NARCISSISTIC MOTHERS?

Dear DONM,

Sometimes close friends really want to understand, and we can struggle to know what to say.

Here is my attempt to explain it (if you find this useful, by all means copy it to give it out to other people):

Narcissistic mothers do the opposite of what real mothers do.

Where real mothers build us up, narcissistic mothers knock us down. They either do it deliberately, for the pleasure of it, if they're malignant narcissists, or just carelessly, as collateral damage to their own wishes.

Real mothers provide a soft place for us to fall, when their daughters are down and weary. Ours begrudgingly provide a barren concrete slab, or maybe a mattress of barbed wire, for the fun of adding to our misery. And they'll never stop reminding us of how they helped us.

Real mothers see themselves and their daughters as being on the same side. Our mothers see us as the opposition or the competition.

Real mothers enjoy our company. Narcissistic mothers enjoy our attention.

Real mothers see their daughters' beauty and applaud it. Ours will make sure we know all our flaws.

Real mothers want their daughters to fulfill all their own potential. Ours do not want us outshining them. Unless they want us to do well as a reflection on them.

Real mothers rejoice in their daughters' successes. Narcissistic mothers resent them. They might milk them, of course, for attention from others. But they'll resent us for doing so well, and any words of congratulations will stick in their throats.

Real mothers have annoying foibles. Ours have toxic and abusive behaviors.

Real mothers mourn for our sorrows. Narcissistic mothers relish the drama of them.

Real mothers delight in their daughters. Ours delight in what we can do for them.

Real mothers are interested in their daughters' lives. Ours have no interest in anything outside themselves.

Real mothers are kind. Ours are completely selfish.

Real mothers are warm. Narcissistic mothers are cold. Except for the heat of anger.

Real mothers hold us in their hearts. Narcissistic mothers hold us in contempt.

Real mothers can be testy and cranky and short-tempered at times. Our mothers are downright nasty.

Real mothers are willing to discuss and compromise. Narcissistic mothers invented my-way-or-the-highway-ism.

Real mothers look for the win-win. Narcissistic mothers insist on the "I win."

Real mothers love their daughters. Our mothers love only themselves.

Hugs,
Danu

HOW DO WE KNOW WHAT
THE TRUTH IS?

Dear DONM,

I spend my life second-guessing myself, always ready to hear the other side of the story and correct myself if I'm wrong. I remember being in awe of my mother and brother at times, because they were always so certain of their rightness. How could they be so certain, I wondered in some kind of admiration, even as I was frustrated by it and how stubborn it made them? I felt that my own fluidity was some kind of personality flaw in comparison. Now that I know better, I think my own uncertainty is better, because absolute certainty is arrogance. But my word, it can get exhausting.

I've struggled with this for a long time: What is truth? How do I know I'm right? Maybe I'm not. After all, the other person is being very certain, and I'm second-guessing myself. How hard should I insist on my perspective if someone else remembers it exactly opposite? I don't have any absolute answers yet, but here are my thoughts on that:

It is a fact that human memory is notoriously unreliable. This applies to everyone, always, but it applies even more when the event to be remembered was a very intense and emotional one (such as some traumatic incident with our narcissistic mother).

What can happen is that we think we remember, and indeed are certain we remember, because the memory seems so clear. The memory, however, can be wrong, especially about details.

So if we witnessed a car crash, for example, we might distinctly recall that the car was white, but in fact it was brown. Or we might recall that it went through a red light when it didn't.

It's not that we're making things up. Well, we are, in a way. It's our subconscious mind making it up, though, rather than us consciously writing fiction. That's why it feels so real. That applies to everyone, but add to it the fact that abused children have a damaged hippocampus, which is the part of the brain involved in creating long-term memories, and we DONMs probably have less reliable memories than most people. So, I feel 100 percent confident in my memories because they seem so real and so right, but I also know that such confidence is misplaced.

What is the truth then? How do I know? Especially, how do I know with regard to events involving my narcissistic mother, when she is adamant that they didn't happen the way I said? I'm no contact with her, but our last conversation included her patronizingly telling me I had a very vivid imagination as a way of denying that certain events even happened. And I have had many, many times when she would say, in surprise and wide-eyed astonishment, "But, Danu, that never happened!" She'd sound so convincing that I'd begin to doubt myself. (Classic gaslighting, of course.)

So what is the truth about anything? How do I know? And of course, by extension, since these letters are really about you, and I only use myself as an example, how do you know?

The fact is that you don't. Not 100 percent. You could be wrong.

But then, so could your narcissistic mother. She is equally prone to remembering incorrectly. Of course, she'll never admit this, seeing as she's a narcissist 'n' all, but it's true. A kind of absolute certainty is arrogance, I think.

So, what I do is to try to get evidence if I can, to back me up. I record things, with my camera or a quick note, if it's important. I compare notes with others who were there to check that I got it right. I accept that I might be wrong. The thing is, I might be wrong some of the time, but I surely am not wrong all of the time. My narcissistic mother was surely not right all the time either.

The truth lies somewhere in between. Since I genuinely was looking for the truth and was only tripped up by the flaws in human memory, and she was determined to deny the truth if it didn't suit her, I think it's fair to suppose that the truth lay nearer my side than hers.

I also accept that while I may not have been right about all my memories, the law of large numbers applies, in that there were many, many events I do recall accurately, and even if we take away an arbitrary 10 percent or 20 percent of them, the pattern still applies and the overall situation was emotionally and psychologically abusive.

I know she has lied (or misremembered, if I am to be charitable) about things I know for a fact were as I remembered them, because I had corroboration for my memory from someone else who was there or some record of the event. So her saying it was x when I recall it as y carries no weight for me at all, even for the things I have no corroboration over.

If someone genuine in my life, such as my son David, remembers something differently to me, then I don't automatically dismiss my own memories, but I certainly don't argue for them either. More likely, he and I will agree to differ on the memory, but discuss calmly and fully whatever the issue was.

So, say I remember him snapping at me, but he says he didn't. We can still discuss how we like to be spoken to respectfully and agree on that. We are discussing it only hypothetically if his memory is right and it didn't happen, but it's still a valuable discussion. He and I don't need to know for sure whose memory is correct. This works because we have a good and healthy and mutually respectful relationship, and each of us values the other, and our relationship with the other, more than we need to protect our ego.

But that, of course, doesn't apply with narcissistic relationships. For those relationships, to the extent that I have to stay in them, I will choose to believe the overall pattern of my memories, even if I know that not every individual memory is correct.

For the rest, I have to come to some kind of peace about the confusion. I have to trust my memories because if you can't rely on anything, that's incredibly stressful, but at the same time, I don't trust them too much. It's a difficult balance and one I haven't quite figured out yet. Perhaps the trick is to be aware of the dilemma and live with it.

There is peace for me in acknowledging the dilemma, though.

Hugs,
Danu

HOW WE CAN GET STUCK
IN THE DRAMA TRIANGLE

Dear DONM,

I've written on the "Daughters of Narcissistic Mothers" website about the "drama triangle" with regard to your narcissistic mother. However, it's true that we DONMs can be on the drama triangle too, and I explore that here. I invite you to read up on the drama triangle on the website to understand the terminology. You'll find it here: www .daughtersofnarcissisticmothers.com/narcissists-drama-triangle/.

A drama triangle consists of a persecutor, a victim, and a rescuer. From the narcissistic mother's point of view, daughters are very often persecutors, but I suspect that it is a rare DONM who is a true perpetrator of violence or abuse toward her mother.

We can end up very stuck in victim mode, though, as well as rescuer mode. With victim mode, it's true that we are victims of this abuser, and because of the brainwashing and a psychological experience called "learned helplessness," we can stay stuck in that mode. So much of the DONM struggle is seeking to free ourselves from the toxic dynamics that keep us as a victim.

We can also be stuck in rescuer mode, as I spoke of before when I wrote about how we feel it's our job to keep our mother happy, and to fix all her problems. This can happen in two ways.

The first is that our narcissistic mother casts us in that role. She makes us responsible for her happiness and well-being. She might even do things such as forget to take essential medication in order to force us into the role of rescuer. This gives her the benefit of playing the victim, and also of getting attention (i.e., narcissistic supply) from us. When we are a rescuer to her, we can feel her temporary approval, as I spoke of earlier, with all the baggage and seduction of that.

The other way we can be a rescuer is to get into rescue mode for others. Being a rescuer is a much higher-energy state than that of a victim. But we surely aren't going to be a persecutor, and we haven't enough healing to leave the drama triangle altogether, so being a rescuer is the only other option.

I can clearly see now that when I first realized my mother was narcissistic, I went into full-blown rescuer mode. I am very embarrassed about that now, in truth, but it was a natural evolution in my healing, as it would be for all of us. There was no malice involved in my rescuing, but from my current perspective, I can see that it was still very dysfunctional in ways.

It takes a lot for me to share this, as I am, rightly or wrongly, embarrassed and ashamed of it. But I try to forgive and understand myself for it, and to know that it was, as I said, part of the evolution of the healing. And I share it in the hope that you can realize this about yourself if you are in the same place.

I like to think, and I do genuinely think, that I have left the drama triangle now. Yes, I am still helping by having the website and the other resources such as this book, but my mindset is completely different. I am no longer so attached to the outcome, I am no longer feeling responsible for everyone's healing, I am no longer getting the same validation from doing it, I'm no longer codependent about it all, and that, I think, is the difference.

To leave the drama triangle, either via time spent as a rescuer or just directly, we need to claim our power, set boundaries, and so on: all the things I have spoken of in these letters. But (and there is no blame attached to this) the victim role can be comfortable. It is seductive. Being a victim, paradoxically, is safe. No matter how awful it is, we know our role, our place. We know the script. We know the steps to that dance without having to think about it. While we are a victim, we have good reasons for why we can't achieve, why our life is a mess, etc.

All of these things are genuinely true; it's not just our perspective. I wrote before about how children of narcissists are bonsai children, and we are genuinely stunted. The difference, though, is what we do once we realize that we are in the drama triangle. We can stay in victim mode or start to grow out of it. But growing is scary. It's the unknown. While we are the victim, everything is the persecutor's fault, but if we grow out of that, we have to start taking responsibility for ourselves.

It is terrifying. I know that. I experience that terror every day, frankly. I am realizing there is a price for everything, and the price for freedom and autonomy and maturity and growth is that we stop being a victim and claim all responsibility for ourselves.

I truly believe it is worth it, but I fully acknowledge how difficult it can be and how scary it is. I often find myself drawn back toward the drama triangle, wanting to feel like a poor little victim or wanting to be a rescuer. I have to be fully aware always of this dynamic, and diligent about avoiding it.

But it is worth it. When I am safely off the drama triangle, I am fully adult, able to make decisions for my own life and steer it in the way I want it to go. I can be a good, helpful friend without letting ego or attachment turn me into a rescuer. I can do my work in a healthy and loving way without getting an ego trip out of it. Satisfaction, yes, of course, but not ego in a dysfunctional sense. All these things are good, and I cherish them, so I diligently monitor myself to make sure I stay off the triangle.

I share this, as ever, in the hope that you, too, might find some direction in this, that you might be able to identify if you are on the drama triangle and, if so, how you might step out of it. Next, I share some ideas for stepping out of the drama triangle.

Hugs,
Danu

SOME IDEAS ABOUT HOW TO STEP OFF THE DRAMA TRIANGLE

Dear DONM,

One thing I've strongly realized about our dysfunctional relationship with our parents, or indeed about dysfunctional relationships in general, is how we get stuck in often-repeated scripts and well-worn grooves of responses. And how a stimulus such as an attack from our mother as persecutor can automatically trigger us into victim mode. Or how a stimulus from her as victim can automatically send us into rescuer mode.

These are all very well-formed habits, and we keep doing them automatically.

The trick to stepping off the drama triangle is to respond differently. To refuse to take the role of victim, persecutor, or rescuer.

I think the best way to stop being a victim is to really own your own situation. You need to effectively announce to yourself: "This is where I am. It absolutely is not my fault that I am here. But from now on, I will steer my own life without apology. I am not obliged to play the part of anyone's rescuer. They are responsible for their own life, just as I am. I do not have to wear the title of persecutor just because someone else tries to allot it to me. I choose to know that living my own life honestly and ethically is not abuse of anyone else, no matter how much they try to spin it that way."

If she tries to cast you in the role of persecutor, saying something like, "You always do x," or "You made me feel y," then instead of defending yourself or apologizing, you can say something like, "I'm sorry you feel like that." Hey, she's not the only one who can do faux-pologies! Besides, you can be genuinely sorry she's feeling distressed without accepting responsibility for it.

If your narcissistic mother tries to cast you in the role of rescuer, you can sidestep that. If she says, "You never do x for me," your automatic reaction might be to point out all the times you did x, or to apologize for the sake of peace and promise to do x more/better in future. But both of those responses accept without argument her implicit belief that you need to do x for her. Instead, maybe brainstorm based on your own mother's particular issues and come up with responses that put the ball back in her court for taking responsibility for herself. Something like, "I'm sorry you feel like that. Maybe you could do x for yourself."

For example, perhaps she creates emergencies to force you to come and rescue her, such as calling you at some ridiculous hour to tell you she forgot to renew her prescription and needs her medication right now. Up to now the pattern would have been that you would drop everything to help her, phoning her doctor or pharmacist to plead with them for help. If you want to stop her from manipulating you into being a rescuer, this has to stop, and you need to let her experience the consequences of her actions as all adults do. If it is something important like medication, I think I would help her one last time, but tell her sternly that it is the last time and she is responsible for this in the future.

Then, the next time it happens, remind her kindly but firmly that it was her responsibility, and let her experience the consequences. Yes, this is very difficult. She could be in genuine medical distress because of this. But assuming she's not suffering from dementia, it is her fault and her problem. It is not your problem. You gave her due warning. It is pure manipulation of her to make you take greater care of her health than she does herself, and if you are to avoid the drama triangle, you need to refuse to take the responsibility.

(In practice, in a case like this, I think I would set up an automatic-reminder email at the time so that I was helping but not rescuing. There are services that can do this—just Google "schedule emails" to see your options. I suggest setting it up so that she gets a reminder email before the old prescription expires.)

If you do fall into emergency rescue again (rather than the strategic helping that the automatic email would be), you are playing the role of the victim. This is a fact, not a value judgment. I do not judge you or think you're wrong to do that, and I hope you don't judge yourself either. It's a fact that you are being a victim in that you have to do something that you don't want to do and that is not your problem to solve.

I do not for one moment underestimate how difficult it is to step off the drama triangle. Both her strong desires and your strong training conspire to keep you on it.

If you do step off the drama triangle, will she be happy with you refusing the roles of persecutor and rescuer? Of course not. Far from it. Indeed, your refusal to do these things will be seen as more evidence of your badness as a persecutor. But don't forget that this is only her perception, and you don't have to let it be yours. This is her song, but you do not have to sing it. More about this next.

Hugs,
Danu

A TRICK DERREN BROWN TAUGHT ME

Dear DONM,

Something that inevitably happens with the narcissistic dynamic is that we get into a situation where we keep replaying the same patterns with our mothers. We contribute to that, too, as we have been trained to respond in a certain way. We have learned our script, so to speak. She says or does x, and we say or do y in response.

When we pluck up our courage to call her on something and she gets upset about it, we rush to comfort her. This is exactly what she wanted, as her emotions are pure manipulation to achieve that very outcome. When she gets inappropriately angry, we rush to placate her, which, again, is exactly the point. When she ignores us, we rush around trying to get her to acknowledge us or speak to us again, which, again, is the idea. She has trained or programmed us to respond in certain ways, and we produce those responses without even thinking.

Another way of looking at this is to think of your relationship with her as a game of tug-of-war, and you and she are both clinging to the rope for dear life and pulling. You can try strategies to get stronger and pull harder. Or you can drop the rope and stop playing. She cannot play tug-of-war on her own. She needs you to respond in certain ways. But you can change the script. You can act in a way that breaks the pattern and disconcerts her.

This is based on something I saw the British mentalist and illusionist Derren Brown speak about. I've tried and cannot find a reference, but I recall the essence of it. He suggested that someone trying, say, to steal something from you expects your response to be one of a limited number of options: fear, resistance, panic, freezing, etc. And so, even for a mugging, there is an accepted script that both mugger and "muggee" know and keep to. But what if you change the script? The mugger doesn't expect you to do something silly and unexpected, such as breaking into song and dance. Derren Brown says that such an unexpected response will disconcert the mugger so much that he (the mugger) may well abandon the mugging. The mugger's worldview has been shaken by your inappropriate reaction to the extent that he cannot cope with it.

It struck me that the same thing could apply to narcissistic mothers. If you respond in a different way, it could put a halt to her narcissistic gallop. In a way, it probably doesn't matter what that something different even is, as long as it nudges both you and her out of the preprogrammed script.

Now, this may or may not work. It depends on how vicious and vindictive she is. I often think the best way to deal with narcissists is to pander to them and give in to them until you can remove yourself. Often, there is no winning with narcissists, and you're better not to even try. Proceed with caution with these ideas.

A lot also depends on your personal situation. If you're living at home or dependent on her, it's probably best not to rock the boat. But if you're an independent woman with your own house and life, you have more power.

For example, if she is whining that you don't phone or visit often enough, your normal reaction might be to try to explain how busy you are with your children and job, or to itemize just how often you do visit, etc., to try to get her to understand and acknowledge that you do visit as often as you can.

But remember we spoke before about how narcissists are toddlers? You don't reason with toddlers, as they just don't get it. Same thing here. Instead, maybe experiment with some different responses:

You could agree with her. "You're right. I don't visit enough." This cheerful agreement, when she was expecting denial or remorse perhaps, will disconcert her. She may well snap, "Well, you should visit more then," and you can then perhaps deflect with some whimsy: "Hmmm, 'enough' is an interesting word," you might say. "Who gets to decide what is 'enough,' do you think? I think there's not enough time in the world, and it just gets shorter and shorter."

You could try putting the problem back on her shoulders: "Can you suggest how I find time to visit you more?" Then, ask more questions about her solutions. If her solution is that you give up some volunteer work, for example, you could say, "But how would those shelter dogs get walked and fed?" And if she says, "Someone else could do it," you could ask, "But how would we find someone else?" Again, it doesn't really matter what you're saying; you're just deflecting.

You could try empathizing with her. This might be kind, because she probably genuinely feels that you don't visit enough. "I know you'd love me to visit more. You probably feel quite neglected that I only visit three times a week," etc. Now, she might well accuse you of being patronizing, but she might well soak it up.

Or you could be brusque and refuse to discuss it: "Well, this is how much it is, and that can't be changed." You could even be kind and refuse to discuss it, saying compassionately that this is how it is, and it can't be changed.

My point is that the programmed and endlessly rehearsed responses don't get us anywhere, so it might well be worth trying something else. In other words, drop the rope.

Hugs,
Danu

THE NARCISSISTIC MOTHER WILL NEVER, EVER ESCAPE THE DRAMA TRIANGLE

Dear DONM,

We spoke of the drama triangle and how our narcissistic mothers are in it and have no desire to ever get out of it. This is a powerful example of how they are stuck in life. As long as someone is a victim, they can never improve their situation. Narcissistic mothers live their whole lives like this. They don't want to improve their situation because what would they have to whine about then? How then would they get sympathy and attention? How then would they be able to blame those they see as persecutors?

That would never work for them. And so, they remain resolutely on the drama triangle. They try to get those close to them, such as us, their daughters, to stay on it with them in our allotted roles as both persecutors and rescuers, to allow them to play their role as victim. They need this.

No wonder they protest so long and loudly when we move off the triangle, when we refuse to play the part anymore. If they are victims, they need persecutors of whom to be the victims, and people to endlessly attempt to rescue them from the fallout of their victimhood. The rescuers and persecutors are often the very same people, including you.

Narcissists don't actually want to be rescued from being *victims*, of course. Just from some of the *repercussions* of it. And they don't want the rescues to be too successful because what would they have to feel victimized about then? Yet they want the rescuers to try end-lessly to rescue them.

In this way I kind of feel sorry for narcissists. No, I never forget the damage they do, so my sympathy is very diluted by my revulsion for them. But I can feel sorry for them too, stuck in their endless self-pity and need for approval and, above all, their belief that everything they need is outside themselves. They have no inner resources at all. They are endlessly dependent on others to get what they need and want in the form of approval and attention and pity and whatever else it is.

So I do feel sorry for them. In a way, my pity empowers me and makes them seem smaller. I suggest to you that maybe you could think of them like this too. It's harder to be scared of someone you see as so weak and needy. Yes, they demonstrate that neediness in such a toxic way. But the root is their fear and weakness.

They're stuck in amber, fossilized, never able to grow or expand. They're stuck in their immaturity, their toddler selves. They will never know the joy of being what they need for themselves, of knowing they are enough by themselves and for themselves. I know the rest of us struggle with that too, but at least we can work toward it and know it's possible. They will never even do that.

Because they accept responsibility for nothing, to them it seems all circumstances are imposed upon them and they're the victim.

It works, in some ways. It makes everyone else responsible for their well-being and happiness, and it gives them a stick with which to beat others they think are falling down on that responsibility.

But no matter that they'll never realize it, living in victimhood is not a wise decision. It is announcing to the world and, even more, to yourself that you are helpless. Helpless is not a nice "place" to live. No wonder they are so unhappy. As much as they need this helplessness, I think they suffer from it too.

We are so much stronger and wiser than they.

Hugs,
Danu

HURRICANES AND WINDBAG MOTHERS

Dear DONM,

I was living in London when it was hit by the 1986 hurricane. This was huge news because hurricanes are unheard of on this side of the Atlantic. And I slept through it!

The first thing I knew about it was the next morning when I was awakened by a frantic call from my mother: "Are you okay?"

"Yes," I said, wiping the sleep from my eyes. "Why wouldn't I be?"

She explained about the hurricane, and I told her I was fine. "Don't worry," I said.

"Mothers always worry," she said piously. "It goes with the territory." Even then, that statement sounded false or off to me, but I couldn't figure out why. Now, of course, I realize.

It's easy to say, "I worry." It's easy to make a breathless, excited phone call to sound concerned. It's easy to say the right words. It probably feels good, as a narcissistic mother, to do those things. She probably felt the glow of being a good mother, so concerned for her daughter that she phoned her right away, always worried about her daughter's well-being. She no doubt felt excited at being involved, no matter how peripherally, in one of the biggest events of the decade.

Even better, it required absolutely no effort on her part whatsoever. It didn't require that she listen fully, or put her daughter's needs above her own wants, or accept any wrongdoing, or be in any way less than her supremely selfish self.

That is when I realized that a narcissistic mother can, and often does, talk a very good talk. But there is no substance behind it. This can be yet another confusing aspect for us DONMs. We feel the essence of the truth that there is no concern for our well-being, but we hear the words that aim to give the impression that she cares.

But I think the truth is exactly as I have said: they talk a good talk, but there is only emptiness behind those words. Our job is to listen to actions rather than words. The truth lies there.

Hugs,
Danu

FORGIVE YOURSELF FOR YOUR MALADAPTIVE BEHAVIORS

Dear DONM,

I think it's a fair bet that most of us have messed up big-time in many ways. I know I have. My life, objectively, is a huge mess in many, many ways.

Now, as you read the rest of this, know that although I speak of myself, that is only as a way of being an example. My life is part of the raw material I mine in order to decipher and make sense of being a DONM, and I share it here. But I hope you will read this and apply it to your own situation if it seems appropriate to you.

I have made a huge mess of my life so far. For sure, I have made huge changes for the better over the last few years, but even so, I'm still years behind where I should be. I'm doing things at fifty that I should have been doing at twenty, and those missing years leave a huge gap that can never be bridged. To be fully honest, there are one or two issues that still remain to be resolved.

I know EFT works very well, and while I have used it lots and benefited lots from it, I don't use it as much as I should. I sabotage myself at many turns, both by continuing to do unhelpful behaviors and by not using EFT to help me avoid the sabotage.

It's so easy to berate myself for the mess I've made of my life. I could nearly make a hobby of it, in fact, beating myself up for all my failings and weaknesses and flaws, itemizing them like beads on a chain.

I'm all about personal responsibility. Our narcissistic mothers are the ones who blame everyone else for everything—"You made me do it!"—and it's not a good trait. It's one I seek to avoid fully. It's very important to me that I own my own mistakes. After all, I was the one who made the decisions I made. I was the one who put the first cigarette in my mouth, and so on.

But I think it's reasonable to apportion appropriate blame where it's deserved. Narcissistic mothers kick us and then blame us for limping. Even more, our narcissistic mothers kick us, and then we blame ourselves for limping.

It is true that we are left emotionally and psychologically damaged by this awful upbringing. It's reasonable that we turn to whatever helps us cope with it, whatever we can do to fill the massive holes left in our psyche. It is fully understandable that we turn to addictions to comfort and support ourselves and to be our friends when we can get comfort, support, and friendship nowhere else.

We don't know what we don't know. I honestly didn't know how to do life. I didn't even know that I didn't know, so there was no way to even go looking for the information. I did see that others seemed to be doing life better than I was, but I thought that was because they were *inherently better* than I was. I thought my lack of life skills was my fault. My siblings, who had the same upbringing as I did, seemed to be doing better in life than I was. They managed to figure out what they didn't know and to get the needed information. So where does the responsibility lie?

I don't have any categorical answer; I'm just trying to find my way through it all. I certainly have blamed myself 100 percent, but I think it's fair to say it is not 100 percent my responsibility. My siblings achieved their successes despite their upbringing, not because of it, and that they managed to overcome it doesn't mean it's my fault for not managing that.

I think we DONMs are very hard on ourselves, and we need to forgive ourselves more for whatever's going on for us. To hold ourselves appropriately accountable, but no more. And to strive to find where that point is.

As one DONM wrote to me, "I am finally letting myself off the hook for some behavior that in retrospect was appropriate for the wound I was carrying." I am trying to do that myself, and I would like to throw open that possibility to you too. Forgiving ourselves for our bad decisions doesn't mean giving up in any way. It means moving forward and striving from a place of self-kindness and self-nurture and self-support, rather than self-blaming and self-loathing.

We did the best we could with what we had. We really did.

Hugs,
Danu

FINDING HEALTHY RELATIONSHIPS

Dear DONM,

DONMs can struggle with how to create and recognize healthy relationships. Many DONMs also have huge issues with trust, which compounds this problem. How can we trust anyone at all, when we have been so fully betrayed by our own mothers? If *she* couldn't be dependable, how can anyone?

These issues make perfect sense given our background, the way we were raised with only unhealthy relationships.

In fairness, it's important to say that making friends and navigating relationships are challenges for all humans, not just DONMs. It's part of the human condition, really, as we are a herd animal whose greatest survival skill is cooperation, and as such, we need other humans. At the same time, we are individuals with our own needs and challenges and neuroses, and that's a powerful recipe for relationship challenges. So, as you struggle with this, don't for one minute think you are alone. I did an online search for "how to make friends," and there were over a billion—a *billion*!—search results. Google estimates that 49,500 people search for "how to make friends" per month. DONMs are not alone in this dilemma. How do we solve it, though?

One solution is, of course, to give up on relationships entirely. I can fully see how that is very enticing. There is huge safety in not risking relationships. We will never experience hurt or rejection or betrayal if we do that. But humans are wired to be social beings, and with few exceptions, we do better when we have good relationships. It would be a sad and lonely life otherwise.

We need to learn consciously how to create and keep good relationships. (Yes, yet another thing we have to learn and do consciously when many others get to do it organically and intuitively. But not all people do, for sure.)

In the next few letters I'm going to explore these questions. Know that I'm still figuring this stuff out myself rather than having it all resolved. But this is what I've learned so far.

The first step, I think, is to know that you're a good person, a person with whom people would want to spend time. It's not surprising that it can be hard to know that. Given the messages we got all our lives about how flawed we are, it can be hard to believe that.

As I said before, I recommend tapping (i.e., using EFT with) the following affirmation: "I am not who she said I was." I suggest tapping on each point in turn (as per the instructions), using that statement four or five times a day for a month or two, and see the difference it'll make to your perception of yourself. Your narcissistic mother lied to you about who you are, and made you believe you were unlovable and unworthy and valueless. This simple affirmation, combined with the power of EFT, is designed to cancel out those lies.

The most important aspect of forming healthy relationships with others is to form a healthy relationship with yourself first. You need to learn to value and respect and care for yourself. If you don't think you're worth those things, how can you expect others to think so? In a way, self-love is the goal of DONM recovery, so it's just doing what we needed to do anyway.

The more you can be comfortable with being fully yourself, the better. That does involve risk, for sure, as there may well be people who don't like who you are. But others, I am sure, will be drawn to your authenticity. We can't please all the people all the time, and it's a total waste of time to try.

It's also important to enjoy your own company. Again, how can we expect others to do that if we don't? This does take a bit of a decision and a bit of determination, but it's so worth it. Not only will it make you more attractive to others, but you get to spend 100 percent of your time with someone whose company you enjoy: yourself.

I went away by myself for three weeks last year, and I have to confess to being terrified by the prospect of doing it. Would I be lonely? How would I manage by myself? It was like diving into the deep end, not sure if I'd sink or swim. In the end, I swam gloriously. I read, I wrote, I dreamed, I explored. It was well worth doing, and it mostly banished my fear of solitude. Not 100 percent—I have to keep relearning that lesson and reminding myself that it's okay. But it was a huge help.

Paradoxically, the less you need other people, the easier it is to find relationships. People can smell neediness and react to that. The more you can be full and complete by yourself, and want relationships as an extra to an already full life rather than needing them to complete you, the better.

The more comfortable we can get holding that paradox, the better.

Hugs,
Danu

MEETING NEW PEOPLE

Dear DONM,

Let's start with how to find relationships in the first place. Often DONMs struggle with knowing how to make new friends. How do we approach people?

The trick is to put yourself in situations where you will meet people. I think it's good to do something regular, as it's hard to make new friends from a one-time meeting. Clubs and volunteer groups are a good idea. Websites can be great tools too. For example, www.meetup.com and local Facebook groups can offer ways to meet new people.

Then—talk to people. Not with the aim of making friends, as that'll put too much pressure on you, but just for the sake of talking to them. Chat with people at the clubs and groups you go to, and people you meet during your day (as appropriate). Make it very low-pressure chat, just about the weather or something else casual. You may feel uncomfortable doing this, but it's a skill like any other, and so it'd be good to practice in low-pressure situations. Let yourself get it wrong as part of learning how to get it right.

Show genuine interest in the people you're speaking to, but don't be afraid to share equivalent information about yourself, or it'll end up sounding like an interrogation. Also, a big part of talking to people is getting to know what you have in common. People like people who a) like them and b) are like them. The things you have in common don't have to be earth-shaking, just common points of reference. So, for example, you might ask, "Where do you work?" and when they answer, you find some point of reference about that: "Oh, I used to work just around the corner from there," or whatever. You can then ask them if they know such-and-such a restaurant or such-and-such a person and take it from there. Do an online search for "making small talk" or "making successful small talk" for more on this.

As you talk to people regularly and see them regularly, you might find yourself drawn to one or two who you might like to be friends with. The first question to ask yourself is not so much about whether they'll like you but whether you like them. Watch out for red flags—we'll talk more about that—and choose well.

Then it's time to see if they like you enough to want to be friends outside the club/volunteer group. So, when you're ready, it's good to take the next step, and we talk about that next.

Hugs,
Danu

HOW TO MAKE FRIENDS

Dear DONM,

What do you do when you want to see if someone would like to be friends?

When you're ready to take it to the next stage, I think the trick is to take a baby step toward them and see how they respond.

Invite her for coffee, maybe, or something else light and easy. She will either respond positively or not. If she responds well, then great. Another way I often take the first step toward someone is to invite them to a party I'm hosting, as that's very low-pressure too.

If she's not interested and puts you off, either by a direct "No, thanks" or more casually than that (sometimes it's hard to say no to people, so they might just agree vaguely that "Yeah, that'd be great sometime," without following up on it), that's fine. It's important to respect others' boundaries by not pushing it. If I liked someone I might try once more by saying casually one day, "We never got that coffee, must do that sometime," in a way that lets them pursue it if they are interested and just didn't get around to it, but that puts no pressure on them if they're not interested. If they still don't follow up on it, I don't do anything more. I stay friendly when we meet but don't pursue it. Both for my own pride, frankly, and also for respect for their boundaries. If they're not interested and reject your offer, that's okay. In many ways finding friends is a numbers game. It's no reflection on you that they don't want to be friends. Not everyone clicks with everyone, after all. I know it's hard, as it takes courage to do even that first baby step and rejection is never nice. But the only way to guarantee never experiencing rejection is to never try, and that can be a lonely place.

If someone makes the first move toward you, then of course it's easier. Make sure you really do want to accept the invitation, though; don't feel obliged to get together with someone you don't particularly want to. It's okay for you to be the person who says no.

After the person has reciprocated the first baby step, you can make another step toward them and wait for them to reciprocate that too. So, if coffee went well, you could suggest seeing a movie or meeting for lunch. In a way, it's like a dance as you and she are metaphorically moving toward each other. And all relationships should be reciprocal, so after you give one or two invitations, I think it'd be good to let her offer the next one.

How far will the relationship progress? That remains to be seen as each baby step only brings you to that new place and at any time you, or they, can step back.

Each relationship is a kind of subtle negotiation as you are subconsciously asking: What are we to be to each other? Best friends? Moderately good friends? Good but casual pals, so that you just have fun together with no obligations or responsibilities? Mutual support system without being friends (e.g., two next-door neighbors who take in each other's packages and water each other's plants as needed)?

As these things are not usually discussed formally, it can be hard to know ahead of time how the relationship will work out, so baby steps will help the relationship find its own level.

There's no right or wrong about any of these different friendship levels, as long as each party keeps to the unspoken but very real terms of the agreement and both parties contribute and take equally within that dynamic. We speak more about equal contributions soon.

Also, as I said, in some ways making friends is a numbers game, so it's good to try to be as social as you feel comfortable being so that there is no pressure about any one specific situation becoming a very close friendship. That'd be a lot of pressure for both you and them at a stage when neither of you knows yet how you'll get along. In a way, this stage is a lot like dating, where you are getting to know each other and seeing if you want to take it further. Going forward, we'll talk about deal-breakers and red flags—that is, things to look out for—and after that we'll speak about the issue of trust, to help this process.

Hugs,
Danu

DEAL-BREAKERS AND RED FLAGS

Dear DONM,

I want to talk about both red flags and deal-breakers in relation-ships. To me the difference between these two is that a deal-breaker is something that only has to happen once and I am out of there. Red flags are behaviors that need looking at and analyzing, and which may lead to me leaving the relationship depending on how things progress. They're behaviors that make me pause and consider and analyze. They are possible warnings.

I'm not very good at seeing red flags in the moment. I sup-pose, like a lot of DONMs, I was trained out of registering them or acknowledging them by all the gaslighting and invalidation. I have tried and tried to improve on this but have not succeeded yet. It's as if my brain freezes during the experience, and I accept it unques-tioningly. I am reliving my experiences with my mother, of course, when that happens. It's only afterward that I find myself thinking: "Hannnngggg on a second!!!!" as I revisit whatever the encounter was. I would rather notice these things in the moment so I can deal with them then and there, but as I say, so far I haven't found a way to do that. At least I do notice them soon afterward.

If you are the same, try to get into the habit of analyzing encoun-ters afterward to check for any deal-breakers or red flags, in both your old and new relationships. You will have to do this consciously, given your upbringing.

Does it seem very cynical and calculating to consciously analyze your relationships? I think it's necessary for us DONMs, as I said. And you know, the words *cynical* and *calculating* have a lot of baggage; perhaps we could use better words such as *careful* and *appropriate* and *necessary*.

Perhaps we'll never become naturals at this and will always have to do it at least semi-consciously. In a way, we're like someone learning a second language as adults—no matter how fluent they become, they'll never have the accent quite right, and they'll never be 100 percent comfortable. But they manage well and can communicate, just as we can learn to be alert for red flags until it becomes almost second nature.

These deal-breakers and red flags apply to all kinds of relationships: friendships, romantic relationships, work relationships, and so on.

Also, a lot of these examples will indicate abuse, but not all of them. Others of them will just be situations that are dysfunctional through no fault of the person concerned; it's just that their relationship or life skills aren't up to being a good friend/lover/colleague.

These red flags also take into account that there is no perfection, that even healthy people have flaws.

Also, it might be interesting to look at each red flag regarding your own behavior. You might have some of them as a form of "fleas." (Fleas are narcissistic behaviors that you manifest, picked up from your mother, without you being narcissistic yourself.)

In the following letter I list out my deal-breakers, and in the letters following that, my red flags. Of course, it's a spectrum, and perhaps in the middle of the spectrum are behaviors that some would consider red flags and others would consider deal-breakers, so I invite you to define them for yourself.

Hugs,
Danu

WHAT ABOUT DEAL-BREAKERS?

Dear DONM,

Here are some absolute deal-breakers.

The first is if someone is violent to you. I honestly think there should be no second chances given for that. People who are violent often apologize profusely and promise and swear they'll never do it again. So perhaps it's up to you if you want to give second chances for that. I would not, as I don't think I want to be with anyone who would turn to violence even once. But if you do, let the one chance be the only chance, for sure. If they are violent twice, that is definitely your clue to remove yourself.

The second deal-breaker for me is if someone tried to control me. Of course, it's reasonable that they would hold me to appropriate standards of behavior, but that's not what I'm talking about. I'm speaking about people trying to tell you what to wear, or how to style your hair, or telling you that you laugh too loudly, and so on.

Or, even worse, is if they try to isolate you from others. That's a favorite trick of abusive people, because if you're isolated, you cannot get any support or any perspective different from theirs.

Now, it can happen that a good person sees that someone else is bad for you and wants to protect you. This can be especially so since we DONMs can be prone to having bad relationships already, so it's very possible they are right when they say, "So-and-so isn't good for you." In this case, apply the deal-breaker tests and the red flag tests (which we'll talk about next) to both people, and see if you can find the truth of it.

One clue would be if the person is trying to separate you from one other person, or from everyone. Or if they manage to come between you and one other person, and then they move on to try to isolate you from someone else. Certainly, if someone starts identifying all your friends as being bad, it's a bad sign. (Unless, by small chance, all your friends are bad. But there would have to be huge proof for me to accept that. I think it's far more likely that if someone is trying to separate you from everyone else in your life, they themselves are the toxic person.)

Another deal-breaker for me is someone who doesn't respect boundaries. I might give someone a second chance on this if I think they're just being thoughtless rather than toxic, by telling them clearly, "When I ask you not to do x, I need you to respect that." But they definitely don't get third chances.

Also, watch how they treat people who are in a service situation to them—in other words, people they can get away with being rude to. Do they speak kindly and respectfully to them? Or do they take advantage of the power differential and speak dismissively, rudely, or even abusively? To me that would be, and has been, an absolute deal-breaker rather than just a red flag.

Another deal-breaker for me is if they are a drama queen or king. I have written earlier about drama queens, so I won't belabor it here except to reiterate that it is definitely a huge red flag bordering on a deal-breaker. If you get involved with a drama queen, you'll be relegated to a supporting role in the soap opera that is her life rather than being an equal partner in a healthy relationship.

These deal-breakers work for me and give me a very clear sense of who I allow into my life and who I don't, and I hope you will find value in them.

Next, we'll talk about the less absolute and maybe less serious red flags. We have discussed some of these behaviors before, but this is to have it all in one place and to make it very clear that they are red flags to watch out for.

Hugs,
Danu

RED FLAGS: PART I

Dear DONM,

Over the next few letters, I'm going to speak of red flags: in other words, behaviors that are not automatically deal-breakers but that absolutely bear analyzing and considering.

In some ways, red flags are tougher to deal with than the deal-breakers, as they're more subtle. But they're essential to consider, as we DONMs can be prone to attracting more narcissists into our lives than others do. It makes sense as we are primed for this kind of relationship, and so we need to be cautious and careful. If I see these flags, I don't automatically walk away. Instead, on the surface I continue just as I would if there were no flags. But I am gathering information, and I don't commit myself either in practical terms or emotionally until I can perceive the person better and decide for sure.

I have broken this information into three sections as it's long—there's a lot to discuss, and it's all important information. And so to begin:

Be wary of people who try to get too friendly too quickly, and who want to be your best friend/soulmate/lover too soon. Now, of course sometimes people just click. I have a friend of twelve years' standing, and the first time we were introduced, we fell into each other's arms like long lost friends; it's a very happy and healthy friendship. So it absolutely can work.

But toxic people often try to seduce you (in the broadest sense of the word, not just sexually) very quickly, as they don't want to waste too much time or energy getting you into their web, so that is definitely a red flag to watch out for. Don't feel pressured into responding—take things exactly at the speed you are comfortable with. That'll give you good information, because if they respect that, it's a good sign, but if they push regardless, that's a bad sign that shows they're willing to ignore your boundaries.

Similarly, be wary if someone is "too perfect" for you, if you feel like they're your soulmate, if they just "get" you and understand you like no one ever did before. Again, this can happen totally naturally and genuinely, but it's also very likely that this is a narcissist or someone wanting to seduce you into their web.

It works like this: Remember I said that we like people who (a) like us and (b) are like us? Abusers can use this trait deliberately (albeit perhaps unconsciously). So they will be all over you, expressing their admiration and respect for you to make you think they like you.

And they'll do their best to make you think they are like you. So you'll be amazed at how much you have in common, from big things like life values, down to small details like their taste in music. If you hear them say, or find yourself saying very often, "No! Seriously? That's my absolute favorite too!" that can be a red flag. It might not be—let me stress that; it could be fully genuine. But my suggestion is that you proceed cautiously until you know. Balance is the key—don't share too much intimate or private information too quickly. Don't do something in that way that could cause problems for you later. And be wary if they share too much private stuff too quickly with you. It could be just that they are over-sharers in an innocent way, or it could be that they're trying to quickly create an artificial intimacy.

Likewise, I am often wary of people who are extremely charismatic. Now, of course there's nothing wrong with people who are genuinely charismatic, and some lucky people just are. But sociopaths and narcissists can cultivate a kind of manipulative charisma, and at first glance I don't know which category a newly met charismatic person falls into. Narcissists will give themselves away before long, for sure, because their charisma and interest are specifically focused on you, and they cannot manage that for very long.

Be wary of those who put you on a pedestal and declare that you are just absolutely perfect, the most wonderful person they have ever met, etc., etc. Narcissists can do that deliberately, the better to seduce you in what's called "the idealization process," and also because you'll fall even harder when they get to the stage of the game where they start criticizing everything about you, which is called "the devaluation process."

And people who suffer from borderline personality disorder may genuinely think you are perfect, as they are extreme black-and-white thinkers, thinking that someone is all good and perfect until that person makes one mistake and then becomes (in their mind) totally evil incarnate.

Regardless of why they're putting you on a pedestal, it's not a healthy dynamic at all. So anyone who praises you in superlatives is a bit suspect. It's nice if someone admires us, and indeed, if they don't find value in us, then why would they be with us? But excessive praise and adoration is definitely a red flag.

As we discussed before, if one friend doesn't like this new person, it could be that the original friend is the toxic one not wanting you to access someone healthy and good for you. Or the original friend could be right about the new person being bad for you. Judge this circumstance on its own merits, I suggest. But if a large percentage of your friends don't like that person, that's definitely a red flag.

Another red flag is if anyone runs you down or demeans you. For sure, they can disagree with you, and it's fair if they call you on inappropriate behavior. But they should criticize your behavior (if it's justified) and not your personality. In other words, they should comment on what you do rather than who you are. And any criticisms should be aimed at solving a problem rather than making you feel bad. For sure, even well-meaning people can have poor skills like this, so it's not an immediate deal-breaker, which leads me to the next point.

They should be open to criticism themselves, as long as you do it calmly and fairly. So if they are criticizing you in negative ways, they should be willing to listen to you when you ask them to criticize you in healthier ways.

Hugs,
Danu

RED FLAGS: PART II

Dear DONM,

Here are some more red flags for you to consider when you think of relationships both old and new:

In good relationships people should be willing to listen to and honor your complaints. (Of course, it is your responsibility to make sure the complaints are both fair and expressed calmly and kindly.) Someone who invalidates you or gaslights you or dismisses your complaints is not a healthy person to be around. Their listening to you doesn't automatically mean they agree with you, and that discussion might lead to compromise, or to you seeing their point of view. But the discussion should be an open and honest and respectful one in which your concerns are taken seriously.

They should operate a healthy "friend-account balance," having deposited enough good things into the friend-account before they draw on it. And by that I mean, for example, that a new acquaintance should not be leaning on you for support when you and she have not built up that level of friendship. This is an aspect of becoming too intimate too quickly, but also of taking advantage of you. Long-term friends can certainly depend on you, perhaps even over months if needed—for example, during a marriage breakup or a health problem. But there will be a lot of friend-currency in the bank account already, in terms of times they listened to you, babysat your children, included you appropriately in their celebrations, etc.

Another red flag is if you feel exhausted and down and depleted after having been with them. In a healthy relationship you should feel good and energized and happy after being in the person's company. This is one for which there are exceptions: If a good and long-term friend, who has a good friend-account balance, is going through a tough time and leaning on you for that, you will probably feel tired and worn out after being with her, and that's understandable and appropriate. But if you feel depleted after every encounter with someone, that's definitely a red flag.

There should be roughly a 50/50 share of relationship work. By which I mean they will call or text you approximately half the time, seek out your company about half the time, and so on. Conversation should be roughly 50/50 too. These things aren't an exact science, and I'm not saying you should keep track and refuse to phone someone because you phoned last time. But if it's always you doing the work of managing the relationship, then that's something to look at.

They should be willing to do favors for you. Appropriate favors, of course. You wouldn't ask a new acquaintance to lend you a large sum of money or pick you up from the airport in the middle of the night. But you can ask favors appropriate to the levels in your relationship-account. It can be a good way to test someone, actually, to ask them to do you a favor. Narcissists and other toxic people will not like that, and their reaction will give you a lot of information. They might do the favor but immediately extract a much bigger favor back from you. Or they might agree to it and then somehow "forget." Or they might wriggle out of it entirely. Now, no one *has* to do you any favors, and if someone decides not to, that's them setting a healthy boundary. But it also tells you the level of the relationship, and that's fine too. If they're refusing to do favors and yet wanting to know you better/be better friends/be lovers, etc., that is not right.

They should respect you. This means respecting your time, your feelings, your property, your autonomy, and so on. If they are careless with those things, it is a red flag.

Especially, they should always speak respectfully to you. Even if they disagree with you, they should speak respectfully. Even if they shout angrily or in frustration, they should do so respectfully. "I am sooooooooooooo fed up with you doing x" is acceptable (of course, the less you can get to that level of argument, the better). "You're a stupid cow" is not acceptable.

Do they have any long-term relationships? It's a big red flag if they don't. Now, there can be good reasons for that—DONMS, for example, may find they have to start fresh with all new relationships when they realize all their old ones were toxic, and that is no reflection on the DONMs as people. So it's not an automatic deal-breaker, but it's definitely something to consider.

Along the same lines, how do they speak of people from their past? There can be hurt and anger, for sure. But is their tone vindictive and nasty? Do they accept any of the responsibility for what went wrong?

In general, do they own their mistakes and their flaws? Or is everything always the fault of someone or something else? If that's the case, you won't be surprised to hear, it is a huge red flag.

Hugs,
Danu

RED FLAGS: PART III

Dear DONM,

One of my biggest red flags is when people speak *at* me, not *to* me. This is a subtle thing but very real, and I bet you know what I mean. You can feel it even if you can't exactly pinpoint the difference. You are an audience, not a co-conversationalist. The speaker is engaged in a lecture rather than a conversation. They don't read any of your cues because they're not engaging with you at all.

I hate it when it happens. It feels so incredibly depersonalizing, as if they are eroding my whole personhood and I am nothing to them but an audience. Now, I have no problem listening to people—I'm known as a good listener. I even have no problem with someone who talks a lot (as long as they'll listen in turn when it's important too). But someone who talks at me is not someone I want or need in my life at all. It makes perfect sense, really, because of course, to my narcissistic mother I was nothing but an audience. She (and my father too) spoke at me rather than to me. I often felt like a cardboard cut-out image of me, rather than my real self, when I was with them. So yes, anyone else doing this to me definitely raises a red flag.

Another red flag is if they see you as flawed and try to fix you. There is nothing wrong with holding you to a reasonable standard of behavior, but if they see you as a project in need of fixing and it's their job to do it, that's not a healthy dynamic. Honestly, if they see you as that flawed, they'll be better off without you, and you'll definitely be better off without them. Being their project will be death to your self-esteem. It's also very toxic, as it means they will be controlling you and micromanaging, and that's not good on all sorts of levels.

Likewise, if they are someone you feel the need to fix, then it's not a good relationship. As we spoke about before regarding the drama triangle, you might get stuck in the role of rescuer, which is not healthy for them or you. If they're that damaged, honestly, you need to walk away. You're probably not a therapist, and even if you are, using those skills in personal relationships to fix someone isn't healthy. And as a DONM you most likely will have enough work sorting yourself out without trying to fix others. I know that fixing others is a good distraction from dealing with your own stuff (go on, ask me how I know—I have felt that pull for sure in my own life), but it's not healthy.

Sometimes we have to walk away from unhealthy relationships. But if someone uses that threat as a way to manipulate you, it's toxic. Again, there are shades of gray here. If you are drinking too much or abusing drugs, and a friend or partner gives you an ultimatum that you have to get sober/clean or they'll have to leave, I don't think that's manipulative. That's fair warning. That's trying to get you to realize how serious this is.

But if someone is constantly threatening to leave for all sorts of smaller reasons, as a way to manipulate and control you, that's a form of coercion and bullying and control, and it's not healthy. This is a very serious red flag and in fact, I would argue, a deal-breaker.

If you feel you have to hide your true self in their company, that's a red flag too. Now again, I have to qualify this. We all put masks on sometimes, and that is appropriate. One of the ways in which we grow closer to people is to drop some of the masks. But in their company, do you feel like you are still you, just wearing a socially appropriate mask (which is fine), or do you feel you have to pretend to be not you (which is not fine)? It's subtle, I know, but if you tune in to your body and ask yourself that question, you should be able to feel the answer.

So there you have it—a long list of red flags to look out for. It might seem overwhelming to monitor all of these, but try not to let it feel like that. Like any skill, the more you practice it, the easier it'll become.

Hugs,
Danu

BUT WHO CAN YOU TRUST?

Dear DONM,

DONMs often write to me that they struggle with trust issues. They might avoid friendships and other relationships because how can they possibly trust anyone when their primary relationships—such as the one with their mother—have been toxic and abusive? And like most DONMs, they've been let down by other relationships too. No wonder they might want to avoid relationships altogether. And even if they don't avoid other relationships, how do they learn to relax with the relationships they have? They don't want to be tense and distrustful all the time.

I have thought a lot about this, especially since I, of course, deal with these issues myself. I recently experienced a very big betrayal by a long-term friend, someone I trusted completely, who let me down very badly. I am still reeling from that. How can I trust again when even she let me down?

So, here are my thoughts on this, and I hope they may be of some use to you:

I think there are three elements to this, and in a way, it's about defining "trust" differently. Or perhaps "allocating our trust differently" is a better way to put it.

The first is to trust your discernment. We have spoken at length about deal-breakers and red flags, and how being conscious and aware of relationship dynamics can help you allow only healthy people into your inner circle. This means that you are automatically picking more trustworthy people, and therefore, it makes sense to trust them more.

The second way of looking at trust involves a kind of paradox. Let me explain by speaking of something else first: there is a paradox in how we live our daily lives. We consciously know that tragedy can strike at any time. Disaster can come out of the blue to change our lives irrevocably. The odds are pretty good that it *won't* happen, but the odds aren't zero.

However, we live our lives on the basis that those odds are zero. This is why people who have experienced disasters say, "You never think it'll happen to you" or "Why me?" We believe we are somehow shielded from disasters that can befall others.

I'm not criticizing this, you understand. At a very deep level, it's a necessary psychological trick, or we'd never function at all. If we allowed ourselves to truly acknowledge how precarious life is, we'd cower in our beds, never getting out, and then probably die of thrombosis.

In order to live any kind of a quality life, we have to take risks. Each person gets to decide for herself what risk/safety ratio she's comfortable with, which is as it should be. But no one takes zero risks. Everyone goes out into the street even though accidents can happen there. Everyone eats, even though choking to death is a very real risk.

And here is another point: No matter how much we like to think we can live our life in safety, the fact is that we will die. Ultimately, we are absolutely not safe. This story only has one ending. And yet, we live as if we will not die. Again, we have to, for sanity's sake.

And so we live in a kind of half-aware paradox in which we know there is a good chance we are not safe today, and there is zero chance we are safe indefinitely, but even so, we live as if that weren't the case.

I think this is the healthiest way to approach relationships. Yes, do your best to choose good relationships, just as you do your best to live a safe life by taking sensible precautions. And keep that kind of semi-alertness we do when we drive, where we aren't tense with fear and panic in every moment, but we are ready to snap to attention if a situation arises. As we drive, our subconscious is continually scanning our environment for us, ready to be alert if needed, but we don't have to consciously think of danger in every moment. The same thing can apply with relationships.

If clues arise that something isn't right, don't ignore them, but at the same time don't fret otherwise. Trust that your relationship is good, just as you trust your journey by car will be safe. Know, too, that all relationships will end, just as all lives end, whether by death or by breakup. I know it's hard to acknowledge, but this is the reality we live with. And so, when a relationship ends, know that it's just part of the flow of life.

Hold your relationships lightly. Live as if the person definitely won't leave you, while knowing that they might. As I said, it's a paradox. Same as you know you'll be safe in your daily life and at the same time that you might not.

And then, the third aspect to trust is this: Trust in your own resilience. Trust that even if people do let you down, you'll be okay. We'll speak more of this next.

Hugs,
Danu

BUILDING RESILIENCE

Dear DONM,

We mentioned in the last letter about trusting in your own resilience. I think this is an essential aspect to navigating in the world, with regard to relationships and everything else too.

And so I think a lot of the work we need to do day-to-day is in building resilience. It's something we need to build ahead of time so we have it when we need it. Here are some thoughts on how to do this:

Self-care is important for this: eating well, exercising, getting enough fresh air, getting enough sleep, and so on. It's hard to deal with problems when you're feeling under the weather.

Try to keep a sense of humor about life and its problems. I always try to remind myself that life is important, but it doesn't have to be serious. There can be a kind of strength in dry humor. This is one of my strengths, I believe, and I can promise you it has saved me on more than one occasion. Humor really does help you cope if you can cultivate it.

Apart from finding the humor in your bad situation, try to take breaks from that situation by laughing in other ways. Watch comedies, for example. Laughter is so very healing for us.

Another way to take breaks from a bad situation is to do things that require effort and/or concentration so that you cannot think of your issues—running, housecleaning, painting, etc.—whatever you would like to do that will just give you a break from the stress of it all.

As described before, in the section about how a cycling hint helped me, take baby steps to solve the problem. Know that this, too, will pass. The pain will ease.

And yet again I remind you about EFT. EFT helps in times of crisis and upset to ease the emotions, to help you handle really tough things. I find I can approach life with more confidence knowing I have this way of soothing and calming myself.

As we discussed before, another way (and this one is harder and for me is definitely a work in progress) is to become less attached to any specific person or circumstance. To work hard having your own happiness be a thing unto itself, not dependent on outside circumstances. To stop putting conditions on happiness, in other words. The only source of unhappiness is when reality is different from the way you want it to be, and there are two ways of solving that: change reality so it's the way you want it to be, or change your wants so they align more with reality.

This isn't about giving up all desires or wants or wishes. A lot of the fun of life comes from identifying and going after wants and desires. I definitely have a very healthy wish list for circumstances I want in my life, both small and big!

But the trick is to *want* these, not to *need* them. To want them and strive for them in a path kind of parallel to your happiness, rather than a path leading to happiness such that you can't be happy until you get there.

More and more I'm convinced that this is the answer: to decide to be happy regardless. It's not easy, though, and I am only attempting these myself. It's a new skill for me, and I keep failing, but I do keep trying, and yes, my happiness levels are exactly measured by how well I succeed in this.

And so I have come to realize that no matter what happens, I'll be all right. I'll be okay in a way that cannot be defined, as there is nothing to say about it, as it has no conditions. I'll be okay because I *decide* that I'm okay regardless of circumstances. That is resilience, and I think it's probably the quality most worth trying to cultivate. The last few years have been beyond challenging for me, and this is the learning I have gotten out of them. It was hard-won learning, but it's so valuable.

Now, I'm not in some kind of enlightened state where I know this and live it all the time. I do get knocked out of it, for sure. But I keep that knowledge (that I'll be all right) in sight and come back to it as soon as I can after trauma or upset. And to the extent that we can do this, I think we have resilience, and I do so wish that for you.

Hugs,
Danu

PSYCHOLOGICAL ABUSE
VERSUS PHYSICAL ABUSE

Dear DONM,

I have heard DONMs say, "Well, at least she never hit me."

I understand that—I really do. We are looking for any crumbs of relief we can get, any sense that it wasn't that bad. But in a way, when we do this, we are invalidating ourselves. Because the truth is that psychological and emotional abuse are damaging in a very real sense.

Pure psychological abuse, with no physical element, is a terrible, traumatizing experience for a number of reasons.

The first is that you don't even know it's going on. I describe this in my first book, *You're Not Crazy—It's Your Mother*, when I discuss narcissistic abuse being a hidden abuse because we don't even know we are being abused. If you are being physically assaulted, you know it's happening. Psychological abuse can be so subtle and subliminal that we don't even realize it's happening. Because you don't know it's happening, it slips by your defenses and goes straight to your subconscious to become part of your truth—that is, what you believe about yourself. You don't get to analyze it or consider if it's true or not; you just absorb it wholesale, and come to think of yourself as stupid or unworthy or whatever horrible message they are giving you.

Psychological abuse can be, and often is, pretty much constant. The undermining and snide comments, invalidation, gaslighting, and so on—they can happen with the abuser's every breath, nearly. And even if the abuser isn't there, we second-guess ourselves so much that it's like the echo of their abuse.

So please do not dismiss what your narcissistic mother did to you, even if she's not physically violent.

Hugs,
Danu

THIS IS NOT THE LIFE I ORDERED

Dear DONM,

One thing I've been wrestling with about this whole DONM thing is how my life is not turning out how I wish. Obviously, I have no parents in my life anymore. I have a relationship with only one sibling, and that is strained enough. I have written before of how my marriage ended as part of this whole process. I am not really in contact with any extended family. There are other issues too, which are also tough.

My life feels very meager and thin to me, and I find it easy to lapse into feeling very sorry for myself about it. Truly, this is not the life I ordered.

But this is the life I've got. And I can whine about it and throw myself a pity party and concentrate on all that I do not have. Or I can embrace what I have and celebrate that.

There's an Irish proverb, "You never miss the water till the well runs dry," which means, of course, that we take for granted all the good things until they're gone. I am trying to cultivate an attitude of celebrating the good things while I have them—even things we'd normally take for granted.

I remember as a teenager having a really bad throat infection, and literally every swallow was agony. I remember swearing that I'd never take a pain-free swallow for granted ever again. Of course, I failed in that promise.

But now, when I try to celebrate the life I have, I think of that, and think of all the things I can do that others can't—things that are not to be taken for granted. All my physical health, for example, in which swallowing without pain is the least of it.

And I've mentioned before how much I love cycling. I try to really, really appreciate all I have that makes this possible: Enough money to have bought a bike. Enough health to be able to cycle. Living in a place that allows me the cultural freedom to cycle. Living in a low-crime area so that it is safe for me to cycle off by myself. Living in beautiful countryside that is a joy to cycle through. Living somewhere with mild enough weather that cycling is usually possible.

None of these things is a given, and I try to remind myself of how lucky I am to have them all come together to give me the joy that I experience from cycling. I also try to expand these thoughts into all my life.

I fail often, of course. So this writing is as much to remind myself as to share with you. We teach what we need to learn, after all.

When I am tempted to sink into despair about the narrowness of my life, I realize it's only narrow by comparison in a specific direction. Yes, there are people who have far, far more than I do, in all aspects of life. But there are also people who have far, far less, and I am so lucky and privileged in so many ways.

I'm not proud of my self-pity, and often I think it's ridiculous that I fret over all that I don't have and ignore all that I do. I get cross with myself when I start wallowing in self-pity, and I need to stop doing it.

I hope I don't come across as brusque or unfeeling. This is me thinking aloud about trying to find balance—to acknowledge and honor that things are not perfect for us DONMs without dismissing or invalidating that, on the one hand, but to acknowledge and celebrate what I do have, on the other.

And hopefully to inspire you too, if and when you feel down about the whole DONM thing, to celebrate what you do have.

Hugs,
Danu

THE ROAD YOU'RE ON WILL
TAKE YOU THERE

Dear DONM,

The Irish Tourist Board had a slogan a few years back, in pre-GPS days, which was: "The road you're on will take you there." Frankly, I think it was them making a virtue of a necessity, in the sense of: "It's a feature, not a bug!" because, for some reason unknown to us lesser mortals, road signage in Ireland is dreadful. It's not so bad on the big roads, but on the myriad of small country roads it's inconsistent and unreliable. So it's very easy to get lost.

And of course, getting lost can be frustrating, even for an Irish person like me who is used to the system. I can only imagine tourists who come from more organized and efficient countries finding it even more frustrating and annoying. Hence, the Irish Tourist Board trying heroically to frame it as a good thing rather than a problem.

Why am I telling you all this? Well, following from what I wrote about it not being the life I ordered, I think that this motto, "The road you're on will take you there," can be a good one for life.

Because the road we're on is reality. It's a fact. We can't suddenly magic ourselves to a better or different road, no more than we can magic ourselves back in time to make better decisions.

And so, all we can do is to plot the route from where we are to where we want to go. And yes, we might be further away from our eventual destination than we would otherwise have been. But again, that's reality, and all we can do is to go with it. And, too, sometimes we have to redefine the "there" to which we're going. (Hope that makes sense!) I, and other DONMs I know, often mourn who we could have been and what we could have been doing if we had had better parenting. Depending on our age now, we might not ever make it to the "there" that could have been possible.

The Irish Tourist Board was careful not to define where "there" was. They didn't say, "The road you're on now will get you to your original destination." That would have been a foolish promise to make, for sure.

But if we keep traveling, the road we're on will definitely get us to a place other than where we are now. And maybe that "there" will be better than the first intended destination would have been. It will perhaps have its own joys and pleasures, unexpected ones, that we would never have gotten to experience if we didn't take this, the scenic route. The highway is more efficient, that's for sure, but the back roads are more interesting.

And even if this isn't true—even if "The road you're on will take you there" is just hype by the Irish Tourist Board's marketing team, and isn't true—well, I think I prefer to believe it anyway. To live my life as if it's true.

Because I cannot change the road I'm on now. I can travel along it and meet new roads, but I can't start from anywhere else than where I am right now. And I would rather decide that this is a good road than fret over the roads I've missed. I'd rather make the decision to be positive about it. And to travel on this road until I get to a "there" I am happy about. And to enjoy the road I'm on now, with its view and its unexpected gifts.

This is a decision I make. Sometimes I have to remake the decision, over and over. And so I do that too.

Hugs,
Danu

LAST WORDS

Dear DONM,

And so we come to the end of this part of our journey together. I hope you have found some value here to help you travel on in your journey as a DONM. In a way, being a DONM is just an extreme version of the normal human condition: confused, making it up as we go along, compensating for our weaknesses, etc. It's a lifelong journey for us all, and I wish you all the very best for your specific route.

If you'd like to keep in touch, please go to my website: www .daughtersofnarcissisticmothers.com. You can sign up for my Guidebook there, and/or contact me. You might like to check out some of the various resources I have gathered to help DONMs too, such as EFT scripts for you to follow to make it easier to deal with some of the issues discussed in this book. Find out more here: www.daughters ofnarcissisticmothers.com/the-healing-store/.

I invite you also to check out my first book, *You're Not Crazy—It's Your Mother*, as it's a good companion book to this one. It's like DONM 101. More details here: www.daughtersofnarcissisticmothers .com/youre-not-crazy-book/

And, finally, I would very much appreciate if you could leave a review on Amazon for this book. It really does help me spread the word. Thank you in advance for that if it's possible for you.

Hugs,
Danu